PR t CH CH

Jack Masterton

SAINT ANDREW PRESS

Revised and updated in 1993
from the original volume
PRAYERS FOR USE IN CHURCH
first published in 1970 by
SAINT ANDREW PRESS
121 George Street
Edinburgh EH2 4YN

Reprinted 1995

Copyright © Jack Masterton 1993

ISBN 0 7152 0680 X

British Library in Cataloguing Data

A catalogue record for this book
is available from the British Library.

0-7512-0680-X

Typeset in Palatino.

Cover photographs by *Paul Turner* on the theme of churches throughout the seasons. Locations include Inveravon, Fortingall and Rosemarkie, in Scotland; and the photographs have been taken from the book *Sacred Stones Sacred Places*, published by Saint Andrew Press in 1992.

Cover design by *Mark Blackadder*.

Printed by Athenæum Press Ltd, Gateshead, Tyne & Wear

Contents

Dedication—
to Margaret, my wife

Introduction

SAINT Andrew Press first published my book of prayers in 1970. Two further impressions followed in 1971 and 1973, which indicated that a number of people found this kind of book useful.

In the intervening period two developments have taken place in liturgical matters—

First, we have grown accustomed to addressing God as 'You' in place of the time-sanctified 'Thou' or 'Thee'. This usage does not strike us now as irreverent, nor does it encourage an undue familiarity with Almighty God. But the change subtly alters the language of devotion, and seems to require modern speech and word-patterns. Therefore I have tried to produce prayers that have the accent of today, and yet are formal and reverent.

The second change follows a general movement in the Church towards involving lay people in the ordering of worship. Participation is called for, and surely would be encouraged by the use of responses. Therefore I include in this book certain standard responses which congregations could easily learn and use.

Jack Masterton
Edinburgh 1993

Part I
SERVICES
on a THEME

1

GOD *the* CREATOR

THE BIDDING

LET us worship God, who, in the beginning, created the heavens and the earth, and made man in his own image.

And God saw everything that he had made, and, behold it was very good.

Let us pray:

YOU are worthy, O Lord our God, to receive glory and honour and power, because you created all things. The universe, with its stupendous size and splendour, is the work of your hands. The sun with circling planets proclaims your glory. And this earth, which feeds all creatures with its fertile soil, declares your providence. In awe at the bounty and beauty of the earth, we adore you, our God, the Creator of this wonderful world.

O GOD, high and holy, in whose presence even angels cover their faces, in shame we bow our heads before you. No excuse can justify our many and repeated sins. No pious pretending can disguise our envious eyes, greedy hands, and hard hearts, And there is no place to hide our selfishness from you. We are truly sorry, and ask you to forgive us.

Lord have mercy
Christ have mercy

3

Lord have mercy

JESUS said: 'Forgive and you shall be forgiven'.

SINCE we all need God's forgiveness, let us from the heart forgive one another, so that we, repentant and forgiving, may ourselves be forgiven.

ALMIGHTY God, we acknowledge you to be our Creator, infinitely patient with us who fail to fulfil your plans, and spoil your glorious works. Mend, Lord, what we have done amiss, and recreate your image in us which we have spoiled.
    In daily life help us to be
        slow to quarrel with others;
        quick to sympathise;
        reluctant to judge and condemn;
        eager to think the best of our neighbour;
        heedless of praise for ourselves;
        and active in all good works
We ask this in the name of your Son, our Lord Jesus Christ.

OUR FATHER ....

INTERCESSIONS

O GOD, the Creator and Preserver of the human race, we humbly pray for those members of it who greatly need your blessing.

FOR the whole Christian Church we pray that, regardless of the world's indifference, it may boldly witness to your great and gracious purpose in creation.
    And for our own Church we pray that, by the preaching

of your Word, it may persuade many men and women to remake their lives after a better plan, and according to the teaching of Jesus Christ.

Lord in your mercy
Hear our prayer

HEAVENLY Father, we pray for parents who create new lives, and those who tend infants and train children, that they may guard the young from evil, and guide them in goodness.

Lord in your mercy
Hear our prayer

O GOD, whose Son worked with wood and stone in Nazareth, we pray for all who build or make things; all who toil at furnaces, or in factories, or in kitchens, that they may take pride in their handiwork and scorn any dishonesty in their employment.

Lord in your mercy
Hear our prayer

O HOLY Spirit of God, you cleanse and activate the imagination. We pray for all creative writers, artists and sculptors, that they may be stirred by you to produce works of beauty, truth and goodness, and thereby lift the spirits of us all.

Lord in your mercy
Hear our prayer

MERCIFUL God, we pray for your blessing this day
    on those who are sick;
    on those who nurse them;

on those who practice the art of medicine;
on those who research into deadly diseases.

Lord in your mercy
Hear our prayer

ETERNAL God, from you, our Creator, we came at the beginning, and to you we shall go at the last. We hope for your mercy; we trust in our Saviour; and we rejoice in the fellowship of your saints. May such a faith give wings to our souls when we die, and carry us to heaven.

NOW unto God, the great and wise Creator, who made us in his own image, and re-made us in his Son Jesus Christ, be glory, honour and praise now, and for evermore.

Amen

THANKSGIVING

Sursum Corda

Minister:	Lift up your hearts
All:	*We lift them to the Lord*
Minister:	Let us give thanks to the Lord our God.
All:	*It is right to give him thanks and praise!*

Let us pray:

ALMIGHTY God, our Creator, who in love made human beings, and in your wisdom made us of body, mind and soul, we give you thanks and praise.

FOR our bodies and their evolution under your guidance,

and for our five senses which enrich our experience, we thank you, O Lord.

FOR our minds and their developing intelligence, and for the desire to learn more about the world, and to know you better, we thank you, O Lord.

And for our souls, baptised by the Holy spirit, nurtured by priests and prophets, redeemed by your Son Jesus Christ, and sheltered by his Church, we thank you, O Lord.

[To that Church's work in the world we now dedicate this offering of your grateful people.]

And to you, our great Creator and gracious God, be given all honour, glory and praise, both now and evermore.

Amen

2

GOD *the* FATHER

HOW great is the love that the Father has shown to us! We were called children of God: and such we are.

Let us pray:

BLESSED are you, O God, the omnipotent Father, whose heart pities and whose hand guides us all.

Before you we bow in awe and adoration. To you, our Father, we give our love as children. To you, our Creator, we offer our reverence as creatures. And to you, our Lord, we owe obedience as servants. May it please you to receive our humble duty and our praise: through Jesus Christ our Saviour.

HEAVENLY Father, like the prodigal son of old, we come to you with a confession on our lips. We have sinned, O God; we have sinned many times and in many ways. We have been self-seeking envious and greedy. We have fallen short in our duties to you and to our neighbours. But, since we know that your pity and patience are infinite, we dare to ask for pardon.

> *Lord have mercy*
> *Christ have mercy*
> *Lord have mercy*

MAY the Almighty God be merciful to *you*, and, forgiving *your* sins, bring *you* to everlasting life.

MERCIFUL Father, who sent your Son to be our teacher, we have much to learn. Help us, by listening to the teaching of Jesus, to discover the truth, and by studying his life, to gain a revelation of your heart.

LORD Jesus Christ, we remember how you said, 'Love your enemies', and how you forgave those who maltreated you with a cruel crucifixion. Teach us, O Lord, to forgive any who injure us, or insult us, or merely irritate us.

Lord Jesus Christ, we remember how you said, 'Love your neighbour', and how you healed the sick and helped the needy. Teach us, O Lord, to be concerned for those in trouble and be ready to answer every cry for help.

Lord Jesus Christ, we remember how you said, 'Do not store up for yourselves treasure on earth', and how you were

8

content to be poor. Teach us, O Lord, to repress our greed for money and possessions.

Heavenly Father, as we learn to know you better, may we grow to love you more; through our Lord Jesus Christ.

OUR FATHER ....

INTERCESSIONS

MERCIFUL God, and loving Father, we bring before you the needs of the household of the faith, and of your wider family in the world.

PRESERVE and strengthen, O Lord, the universal Church. In particular we commend to your care the Church in this land, a Church deserted by many, supported by few, and weakened by a worldly spirit. Fan the embers of faith in our citizens, and warm the hearts of church members, that we may set about enlarging the church and extending its influence.

Lord in your mercy
Hear our prayer

FATHER of us all, we pray for the millions of people who are hungry, and for the thousands of children who die each day from lack of nourishment or disease. Arouse the sympathy of those cushioned by affluence in the Western world, that they may support every effort to provide food and medical aid to the distressed.

Lord in your mercy
Hear our prayer

REMIND us, O God, that your love, like a father's arms, embraces all your children, whether good or bad, black or white. Prompt us into showing them tolerance, kindness and courtesy.

Lord in your mercy
Hear our prayer

REBUKE, O Lord, those criminal members of the human family who turn life into a bad and brutal affair. Restrain those who abuse alcohol and drugs to gain a fancied happiness. And resist those who pursue political ends with guns and bombs.

Lord in your mercy
Hear our prayer

FATHER, into your hands we commit men and women laid low by a damaging accident, or by a heart-attack, or by the onset of disease. Look after them as you alone can do.

Lord in your mercy
Hear our prayer

WE pray you, Lord, to lift the spirits of all who work every day and all day in their domestic tasks, tending little children, looking after disabled persons, or nursing aged relatives. Give them a glad heart and a sense of humour.

Lord in your mercy
Hear our prayer

ETERNAL God, heavenly Father, in whose presence the saintly people of every age rejoice, we praise you for them all, thanking you especially for those we knew and loved, who have gone from our sight, but who will never go from our memory. Inspired by their example, may we follow in their footsteps on the narrow road that leads uphill to heaven. And there at length may we join the saints in light, through Jesus Christ our Lord, to whom, with you and the Holy Spirit, may praise from all the world be given. Now and for evermore.

Amen

THANKSGIVING

Sursum Corda

Minister:	Lift up your hearts
All:	*We lift them to the Lord*
Minister:	Let us give thanks to the Lord our God
All:	*It is right to give him thanks and praise*

Let us pray:

WILLINGLY we offer thanks to you, O God, Creator of the world, and Father of us all.

For light we thank you, Lord:

> for the powerful light of the sun, and the soft light of moon and stars;
> for the light of human reason; and for your light which, in the Bible, is a lamp to our feet, and in Jesus Christ is the saving light of the world.

For life we thank you, Lord:

> for the life of the body from cradle to coffin;
> for the life of the soul nurtured by your Holy Spirit;
> and for the life we hope to enjoy eternally.

For love we thank you, Lord:
for the love of parents, family and friends;
for the love of other Christian men and women;
and for your love which, like a robe, covers us all.

IN token of our thanks, we make this offering [of alms and] of praise; through Jesus Christ our Lord, to whom, with you and the Holy Spirit, be thanks and praise for ever and ever.

Amen

3

GOD *the* KING

THE sovereignty of the world has passed to our Lord and his Christ, and he shall reign for ever and ever ... King of kings and Lord of lords.

Let us pray:

YOURS, O Lord, is the greatness, the power, the glory, the splendour, and the majesty; for everything in heaven and on earth is yours; yours, O Lord, is the sovereignty, and you are exalted over all as head. Reign, then, in our hearts, O Lord, and bring all the peoples, who live between the poles, under your rule; through Jesus Christ your Son, our Saviour.

O Holy God, throned in glory, we are quite unfit to appear before you. We have not allowed you to rule our lives, or to reign over our hearts. We have withheld the reverence that was due to you, and ignored your royal commands. Although claiming to be citizens of your Kingdom, we have done little to support or extend it. Ashamed of what we are, we dare to appeal for your mercy and pardon.

Lord have mercy
Christ have mercy
Lord have mercy

MAY God speak words of pardon to us, for our trust is in his mercy and love, which he has shown us in Jesus Christ our Lord.

JESUS said: 'How hard it is for the wealthy to enter the Kingdom of God'.

DELIVER us, good Lord, from love of money and the desire to own things, lest we grow heedless of your Kingdom, and unmindful of our duties to you and our fellow creatures.

JESUS said: 'From east and west people will come, from north and south, for the feast in the Kingdom of God'.

DELIVER us, good Lord, from colour prejudice and racial bitterness, lest we try to ban some persons from your Kingdom, and succeed only in excluding ourselves.

JESUS said: 'Not everyone who calls me "Lord, Lord" will enter the Kingdom of heaven'.

DELIVER us, good Lord, from all pious but insincere speech, lest we become hypocrites and therefore unfit to enter your Kingdom.

OUR FATHER ....

INTERCESSIONS

KING of glory, God of grace, in prayer before your throne we remember a needy Church and a needy world.

FOR the Church of Christ circling the world, we pray that, full of faith and love, it may persevere in the work of man's salvation.

FOR the Church in this country, we pray that, weak as it is in numbers and influence, it may be strong in its witness to the Gospel and in its cure of souls.

Lord in your mercy
Hear our prayer

FOR the leaders of this and other nations, we pray that they may find the means to control the powerful, defend the attacked, and punish the aggressor, and thus establish order and justice in this most disordered world.

Lord in your mercy
Hear our prayer

FOR people who suffer under an oppressive government, and for those crushed by secret police, who live day and night in fear of arrest and torture and the execution squad, we pray. May all people of goodwill condemn such inhumanity to man and give aid to the oppressed.

Lord in your mercy
Hear our prayer

FOR signs of the growth of your Kingdom among the nations we pray.

FOSTER, O Lord, a sense of brotherhood;
>   through our sharing of science, music and art;
>   through rescue work done together;
>   and through common concern for wildlife and the green earth.

Lord in your mercy
Hear our prayer

FOR our native land, we pray—this land, where the good seed of the Gospel was sown for many centuries. Lord, change our winter to spring, so that the seed may take root and flourish today, and not be choked by weeds, but produce a good harvest.

Lord in your mercy
Hear our prayer

FOR the countless people who are suffering in body or mind we pray, that you will lift their burdens, or give them strength to bear what they are called upon to bear. In particular we silently name those of them we know and love.

NOW to the King of all worlds, immortal, invisible, the only God, be honour and glory for ever and ever.

Amen

THANKSGIVING

Sursum Corda

Minister:	Lift up your hearts
All:	*We lift them to the Lord*
Minister:	Let us give thanks to the Lord our God
All:	*It is right to give him thanks and praise*

Let us pray:

ALMIGHTY God, King of glory and Lord of life, we praise your great and holy Name, because you have ordained our lives, arranged their circumstances, and set out feet upon the Narrow Way.

DAY after day, O Lord, we have reason to thank you for the morning's light, for more hours to live and labour, and more time to do our duty to you and to our neighbours.

NIGHT after night, O Lord, we have cause to thank you for the evening's shadows, for time to read and see our friends, and for the darkness when, with folded hands and quiet minds, we may rest, or sleep and dream.

SUNDAY after Sunday, O Lord, we have a duty to thank you for the holy day you made, for worship that is a foretaste of heaven, and for time to hear your Word and sing your praise.

NOW to our God, the eternal King, who sits on the throne of the universe, who reigns in our hearts and rules the nations: to him be glory and praise for ever and ever.

Amen

4

GOD *the* JUDGE

THE BIDDING

THE LORD sits enthroned for ever. He it is who will judge the world with justice and try the cause of the peoples fairly.

Let us pray:

ETERNAL God, the Judge of every person and nation, whose word is law, whose judgment is impartial, whose power is great, but whose mercy is greater still—before you we bow in reverence and awe.

Graciously accept the prayers and praise we offer you, in the name of our Lord Jesus Christ.

ALMIGHTY God, you have warned us that we shall all come to judgment one day, therefore prepare us now for that trial. Forbid us trying to deny our guilt, or excuse our faults, or blame others for our failures. We have sinned, O God; we have sinned repeatedly and knowingly and have no defence. We had your Word to guide us, and your Son to follow, and your Holy Spirit to inspire us, and yet we fell from grace. We sinned, repented, and then sinned again. But now we are ashamed and sorry, and beg that you will not treat us as we deserve, but in pity forgive us.

> *Lord have mercy*
> *Christ have mercy*
> *Lord have mercy*

For your comfort, hear these words of a Psalmist:
'The Lord is merciful and gracious,
    slow to anger and abounding in love.'

HEAVENLY Father, so strong are our temptations,and so frequent are our falls, that we entreat you to hear and answer our supplications.

HELP us, O Lord, to control our minds, so that we recognise what is morally right and instantly act upon it.

HELP us, O Lord, to control our hearts, so that emotion does not rush us into rage, or lust, or despair.

HELP us, O Lord, to control our tongues, so that we always speak the truth in love, and use words that encourage our hearers.

HELP us, O Lord, to control our eyes, so that we turn them away from what is base and evil, and focus on what is good and admire what is excellent.

O LORD Jesus Christ, who declared that God will judge us, as a man judges between sheep and goats, grant that, having lived an upright life, we may be herded with all God's sheep, into the fold of heaven.

OUR FATHER ....

INTERCESSIONS

HEAVENLY Father, as love and duty demand, we pray for the world and its people, and for the Church and its members.

18

GOD preserve your Church in this fallen world. May it not weary of proclaiming your law, which judges mankind, condemns wickedness, and censures corruption.

Lord in your mercy
Hear our prayer

JUDGE and condemn, O Lord, those who use rifles and bombs for political ends. Restrain the terrorists, and frustrate their brutal methods. And support all persons unjustly accused and imprisoned.

Lord in your mercy
Hear our prayer

O GOD, the source of truth and justice, guide those who are called to dispense justice, to clear the innocent, and convict the guilty. May each of us, in his or her vocation, think fairly, love mercy and walk humbly with you.

Lord in your mercy
Hear our prayer

O LORD Jesus Christ, who fiercely condemned any who abused children, protect the young from assault by cruel parents or by perverts. Rescue older children from the many evil influences in our society which threaten to poison their souls.

Lord in your mercy
Hear our prayer

O LORD Jesus Christ, who punished the traders by driving them out of the Temple, remind all who are engaged in

19

business in the market-place, or in the city, of their solemn
duty to deal justly and honestly.

Lord in your mercy
Hear our prayer

MERCIFUL Father, to your sleepless care we commend
    all who suffer from disease or disability;
    all whose hearts are sad and sore;
    and all who live in discomfort and loneliness.
And for those about to die, we pray that you will take them
by the hand through death's dark into heaven's light.

Lord in your mercy
Hear our prayer

GOD of eternity, we bless you for the great and glittering
company of your saints; those men and women who, after
their days of trial, were absolved and welcomed into heaven.
Among them we honour the men and women we knew on
earth, who were pillars of Christ's Church, and examples to
us of godly living and faithful service to others. By following
them, as they followed Christ, may we avoid the way to the
everlasting bonfire, and arrive in your heavenly Kingdom;
through Jesus Christ our Lord, to whom, with you, the Father,
and the Holy Spirit, by glory, honour and praise for ever.

Amen

THANKSGIVING

Sursum Corda

Minister: Lift up your hearts

All: *We lift them to the Lord*
Minister: Let us give thanks to the Lord our God
All: *It is right to give him thanks and praise*

Let us pray:

ETERNAL Father, we thank and praise you, because, although you are the Judge who knows all and sees through all excuses, you have dealt mercifully with us. Much to be blamed, we have not been punished; often at fault, we have been forgiven.

WE thank you, Lord, for every gracious influence in our lives, especially for pious parents from whom we learned to pray and sing your praise and read the Bible; and for upright men and women who taught us to respect the truth and value honesty, and warned us that there was no peace for the wicked.

WE thank you too, O Lord, for all saints and servants of the Church; for those who laboured to banish superstition and bigotry from society, and darkness from the minds of the ignorant, and cruelty from the hearts of the wicked.

NOW to the Lord our God
        for his goodness at all times;
        for his presence in all places;
        for his mercy in the past;
        and for his promise for the future;
we give our thanks and praise, world without end.

Amen

5

GOD *the* SHEPHERD

KNOW that the Lord is God; he has made us and we are his own, his people, the flock which he shepherds.

Let us pray:

ALMIGHTY God, the Shepherd of our souls, lead us, who form a small part of your flock, into the pastures of your presence. Prepare our hearts for your worship, our lips for your praise, and our ears for your Word; through Jesus Christ our Lord.

HOLY and merciful God, we have all gone astray like lost sheep. Rejecting your guidance and discipline, we have gone our own foolish way. To the calls of duty, we have turned a deaf ear. To the troubles of our neighbours, we have turned a blind eye. And to your rebukes, we have turned a brazen face. Our behaviour and our conversation have fallen far short of our profession. All this we deeply regret, and humbly ask for your pardon.

> *Lord have mercy*
> *Christ have mercy*
> *Lord have mercy*

HEAR these words of St John:
> 'If we confess our sins, God is just, and may be trusted to forgive our sins and cleanse us from every kind of wrong'.

Believe that and be comforted.

MERCIFUL God, because we are as wilful and wayward as sheep, we need a shepherd's care. If you will stay by our side, with staff and crook, we shall be comforted. Guard us, O Lord, in calm weather and in storm, in daylight and in darkness.

HEAVENLY Shepherd, prevent us, your flock,
    from knocking down moral fences;
    from choosing the primrose path of pleasure;
    and from leaving the road because it is steep.

Protect us, Lord,
    from the disease of doubt;
    from the infection of sickly sheep in the flock;
    and from the wish to run away from you, our Good Shepherd.

GRANT unto us, we beseech you, O Almighty God, that we, who seek the shelter of your protection, being defended from all evils, may serve you in peace and quietness of spirit; through Jesus Christ our Lord.

(Roman Breviary)

OUR FATHER ....

INTERCESSIONS

ALMIGHTY God, in our intercessions at this time, remind us that you desire the salvation of all people in every nation and race.

HEAVENLY Father, increase the missionary zeal of the Christian Church, so that millions, who know nothing of the Gospel, may rejoice to hear of Christ and his love.

Lord in your mercy
Hear our prayer

BLESS, O Lord, the work of the Church in China, Japan and the Far East, in order that great numbers of men and women learn the truth as it is in Christ.

Lord in your mercy
Hear our prayer

PROSPER, O Lord, the Church's work in India and Africa. As people there come to know you better, may they love you more, and develop a stronger will to live at peace with each other.

Lord in your mercy
Hear our prayer

O GOD, the Shepherd of us all, supply the needs of your flock in this country, by feeding the lambs and tending the sheep. Prompt us, in your name, to search for every sheep that is lost. And persuade us to rescue the many black sheep in our land.

Lord in your mercy
Hear our prayer

O HOLY Spirit of God, the inspirer of every good life, be active in our universities and colleges. Take part in the training of those men and women whom the Church has selected to be shepherds over the flock. Remove from them any academic pride, or trace of insincerity. Teach them how to 'hold a sheep-hook', and how to herd a flock; for the sake of our Lord Jesus Christ.

Lord in your mercy
Hear our prayer

O God, gracious and merciful, we pray
    for all who are poor, ill-fed and ill-housed;
    for all whose work is without honour or interest;
    for all who cannot find work, or will *not* work;
    and for all who lie sick in bed at home, or in hospital.

Lord in your mercy
Hear our prayer

WITH all our heart, O God, we thank you that in this dark world and difficult life we can look up to you and to your saints, for light and guidance. You are our Light; without you we would live in perpetual night. Your saints mark the Way; without them we would not travel right, but go astray.

NOW to you the Father, with the Son and the Holy Spirit, one God, be glory, honour and praise now and evermore.

Amen

THANKSGIVING

Sursum Corda

| Minister: | Lift up your hearts |
| All: | *We lift them to the Lord* |

Minister: Let us give thanks to the Lord our God
All: *It is right to give him thanks and praise*

Let us pray:

NOW and ever you are to be praised, O Lord our God, for creating this boundless universe, and for designing this planet earth as a home for mankind.

WE thank you, heavenly Father, for life and the gifts which accompany it, for human speech, a rational mind, memory and imagination, a moral sense and an immortal soul.

WE thank you, too, that with these gifts come joys and fears, tenderness and tears. But best of all, you give us hope; hope of a meaning behind the mystery of life; hope of another day beyond the setting sun; hope of meeting the good and brave who have gone before us. Into that splendid company of your faithful servants, O God, summon us at the last. Into your heavenly flock, O God, receive us, the sheep who were lost but are found.

MAY the God of peace, who brought up from the dead our Lord Jesus, the great Shepherd of the sheep, make us perfect in all goodness; through Jesus Christ, to whom be glory for ever and ever.

Amen

6

GOD *the* SAVIOUR

IT was not to judge the world that God sent his Son into the world, but that through him the world might be saved.

Let us pray:

ALMIGHTY God, merciful Saviour, to whom we look for help, because we are weak, and to whom we turn for pardon, because we are sinners, we humbly pray you to accept our worship, hear our praise, and answer our prayers, for the sake of Jesus Christ your Son, our Lord.

MOST gracious God, we are ashamed to confess that we have tried your patience and grieved your Holy Spirit. We have been absorbed with material things, as if our life depended on them. We have spent far too much time on our own concerns and pleasures. We have thought too highly of ourselves, and been offended when we received small praise. And we, who are not quite honest or truthful, have begun to believe we are saints.

Supply us, O God, with the gift 'to see ourselves as others see us'. Thereafter show us ourselves as you see us. And then forgive those of us who are humble and contrite.

> *Lord have mercy*
> *Christ have mercy*
> *Lord have mercy*

MAY the Lord our God, who is gracious and merciful, forgive

our sins, and deliver us from all our temptations, for the sake of Jesus Christ our Saviour.

ALMIGHTY God, we lament what is past, and are resolved to do better in the future. But, because we are weak and liable to sin, we need your strong and constant help. In particular, we beg you to save us from the Seven Deadly Sins.

From pride and an arrogant spirit;
Save us, O Lord
From wrath, a sharp tongue and an evil temper;
Save us, O Lord
From avarice, and an excessive love of money;
Save us, O Lord
From envy of the wealthy and important persons;
Save us, O Lord
From lust of the flesh and lascivious thoughts;
Save us, O Lord
From gluttony, and greedy eating and drinking;
Save us, O Lord
From sloth, and a listless, joyless state of mind;
Save us, O Lord

OUR FATHER ....

INTERCESSIONS

MERCIFUL God, grant that in our intercessions there may be present in our minds your great love for all your children, and your wish that none should perish.

FOR the world-wide Church, O Lord, we pray. Make its members an effective army of salvation to oppose pagan forces.

Call many recruits to its ranks; recall the stragglers; and rouse us all, as with a trumpet-call, to follow Christ, our King and Saviour.

Lord in your mercy
Hear our prayer

O GOD, who sent your Son to a corrupted world to save sinners, we pray for the conspicuous sinners in society. Rouse the sleeping conscience in thieves and swindlers. Break the chains of drug abuse, or sexual perversion, which enslave many. And remind all these lost souls that Christ the Saviour seeks them.

Lord in your mercy
Hear our prayer

O LORD Jesus Christ, you calmed the wind and the waves on the Sea of Galilee. We, therefore, commend to your care those who sail on our stormier seas. Save them from the violence of the sea, and the danger of a rock-bound coast, and pilot them safely to harbour.

Lord in your mercy
Hear our prayer

O LORD Jesus Christ, who in your public ministry, healed many who were sick, let your gracious work continue today through the skillful hands of surgeons and doctors, nurses and physiotherapists.

Lord in your mercy
Hear our prayer

O LORD Jesus Christ, who fed a crowd with loaves and fishes because they were hungry, grant us your concern for those who lack food, or suffer from famine. Increase in all nations, O Lord, a greater sense of brotherhood, so that things are shared more fairly.

Lord in your mercy
Hear our prayer

O LORD Jesus Christ, who caught hold of Peter when he was beginning to sink in the water, rescue all men and women who feel themselves sinking in a sea of troubles, and save any who are tempted to drown themselves in bitter despair.

Lord in your mercy
Hear our prayer

ETERNAL God, we bless and thank you for your saints, the memory of whom has often saved us from giving up, and the thought of whom, standing round your throne in glory rejoicing, has often encouraged us to continue. Following them, in the way they followed Christ, may we reach that heavenly place where the traveller's journey is done.

TO you, the King of saints, the Lord of life and love, God in three persons, Father, Son and Holy Spirit, be given all praise now and to the end of the world.   *Amen*

THANKSGIVING

Sursum Corda

| Minister: | Lift up your hearts |
| All: | *We lift them to the Lord* |

Minister: Let us give thanks to the Lord our God
All: *It is right to give him thanks and praise*

Let us pray:

HEAVENLY Father, with glad and grateful hearts we thank you for our life in this wonderful world you created; this world which, with its plants and trees, fruits and flowers, is as lovely as the Garden of Eden, but, like that garden, has evil present and active in it.

AND we thank you, gracious Father, for our new life, rescued from the power of evil, reborn and re-made by your Son's saving life and death.

WE thank you also, Father, that, because of our costly salvation, human life can be made better and kinder, and that troubles and sorrows can become means of grace, wells of hope, fountains of joy, and intimations of immortality.

NOW to the One who can keep you from falling and set you in the presence of his glory, jubilant and above reproach, to the only God our Saviour, be glory and majesty, might and authority, through Jesus Christ our Lord, before all time, now, and for evermore.

Amen

7

GOD *the* SPEAKER

THE grass withers, the flower falls; but the word of the Lord endures for evermore.

HEAR now what the Lord is saying to each of us.

Let us pray:

YOU, O Lord, are the Word, the Truth, the living God. With attentive minds and listening ears we bow before you, whose voice can be heard over all the earth in the Ten Commandments of Moses, in the preaching of the prophets, and in the teaching of Jesus Christ, the incarnate Word.

Speak to us now, O Lord, in this time of worship; speak words of rebuke, or comfort, or encouragement, according to each person's need; through Jesus Christ our Saviour.

O HOLY God and merciful Judge, we are ashamed to remember, and unable to forget, that we have much to confess to you. Had we listened to your voice in our conscience, we should not have gone astray. Had we read and heeded the Bible, we should not have wasted our time and played the fool. And had we obeyed the words of the prophets, or the appeals of Jesus Christ, we should have been far better men and women today. Therefore, with all our heart we regret our inattention, repent of our wrong-doing, and pray for forgiveness.

Lord have mercy
Christ have mercy
Lord have mercy

JESUS said to the man, 'Take heart, my son; your sins are forgiven'.
In your mercy, speak thus, O Lord, to your servants.

LET us remember Samuel's prayer: 'Speak, Lord; thy servant hears thee'.

O GOD, hush the noise of our busy lives, and smother the urgent whisper of our lust and worldly desire, so that we can hear your voice and obey what is said.

LET us remember Jonah's prayer: 'Lord, take my life; I shall be better dead than alive'.

O GOD, save us from growing angry at your kindness to strangers, or becoming bitter when our wishes are not granted.

LET us remember Christ's prayer: 'Father ... take this cup away from me. Yet not my will but thine be done'.

HEAVENLY Father, give us grace to accept whatever is your will for us. Then, supported by faith in your love, we shall not shrink from drinking life's cup, even when death is in it.

OUR FATHER ....

INTERCESSIONS

OUR heavenly Father, help us now to pray with loving concern for members of your widely extended family.

O LORD our God, may the Church today listen when you speak to it, either to rebuke us for infidelity, or to rouse us to greater activity. May the eager preaching of the Gospel, and the example of devout Christians persuade many to become disciples of Him who is their Saviour and ours.

Lord in your mercy
Hear our prayer

WE pray, O Lord, for all who use the spoken or the written word:
for politicians, that they may not mislead their listeners;
for journalists, that they may study to be accurate;
for teachers, that they may put truth and goodness first;
and for leaders of Unions, or protest groups, that they may speak peaceably, and disdain to use rabble rousing methods.

Lord in your mercy
Hear our prayer

WE pray, O Lord, for all sufferers:
for those who cannot speak, or write, or move,
that they may receive kind attention;
for those mentally disabled by senility, or a stroke,
that they may improve with skillful nursing;
for those in pain from broken bones, or a broken heart,
that they may be comforted.

Lord in your mercy
Hear our prayer

O GRACIOUS God and most merciful Father, who hast given us the rich and precious jewel of thy holy Word; assist us with thy spirit, that it may be written in our hearts to our everlasting comfort, to reform us according to thine own image and increase in us all heavenly virtues; for Jesus Christ's sake. *Amen.*

(Edward VI: 1537-53)

Lord in your mercy
Hear our prayer

INTO your hands, O Father, we commit the souls of those who are soon to die. Attend them as they set out on their journey, consoling them with words of peace and promise.

Lord in your mercy
Hear our prayer

FOR your saints we thank you, O God; for prophets and apostles, preachers and scholars, who spoke and wrote in your name; and for all who proclaimed the Gospel in foreign lands and among unfriendly people. May we live more bravely because of their example and continue your faithful servants unto our life's end; through Jesus Christ our Lord, to whom, with you, O Father, and the Holy Spirit, be glory and praise for ever and ever.

Amen

THANKSGIVING

Sursum Corda

Minister: Lift up your hearts

All:	*We lift them to the Lord*
Minister:	Let us give thanks to the Lord our God
All:	*It is right to give him thanks and praise*

Let us pray:

THANKS and praise are your due, O God, our heavenly Father, because you have never lost patience with the human race, never left us to our own devices, and never ceased to speak to us in love, or appeal, or rebuke. Give us grace, O God, to listen to you.

WE bless you, O Lord Jesus Christ, Son of God, for sharing our human life, speaking words full of grace and truth, and proclaiming the Kingdom of God. Most of all we thank you for taking the burden of our sins upon you, and at the last dying for us on the Cross. You have been kind beyond all expectation and generous beyond all our deserving. Therefore, with heart and voice we praise and thank you, Father, Son and Holy Spirit for ever and ever.

Amen

8

GOD *the* SEEKER

JESUS said: The Son of Man has come to seek and save what is lost.

He also said: I am the good shepherd.

Let us pray:

ALMIGHTY God, we worship you, the shepherd of our souls. You have sought us when we wandered, searched for us when we were lost, and rejoiced when you found us. For this great mercy we thank you. Keep us ever in your fold; never let us go, for the sake of your Son, our Saviour, Jesus Christ.

MERCIFUL God, whom only the pure in heart can see, make us aware of the things which veil our eyes, and darken our hearts. We confess our foolish pride, our ill-temper, and our pretence to be much better than we are. Generously dealt with by you, we have given a mean and grudging response. Repeatedly forgiven by you, we have been slow to forgive others. And, directed to take the narrow way that leads to heaven, we have often stepped aside. Father, forgive us.

Lord have mercy
Christ have mercy
Lord have mercy

MAY Almighty God grant you pardon and remission of your sins, time to amend your life, and the grace and comfort of the Holy Spirit.

Amen

ALMIGHTY God, you are the seeker and we are the sought, therefore give us grace to welcome your search and not hide from you, and to answer your call and not run away.

WHEN we have been caught in a lie,
or discovered in a mean action;
or found to be a hypocrite
seek us out, O Lord, and rebuke us.

WHEN our conscience has grown a thick skin;
  and we can scarcely tell wrong from right;
  and we become obstinate in error;
seek us out, O Lord, and correct us.

WHEN we attempt very little and fail much;
  and we grow old and complain about life;
  and we grieve over departed friends;
seek us out, O Lord, and encourage us.

OUR FATHER ....

INTERCESSIONS

HEAVENLY Father, grant us compassion as now we pray for people in need all over the world.

YOUR Spirit, O Lord, has wonderfully kept the Church alive in a dark and disordered world. Rouse it to greater activity so that many, who have long known and not heeded the Gospel, may find it claiming their interest and touching their conscience. Open blind eyes and deaf ears that the Church may convert many souls.

Lord in your mercy
Hear our prayer

REBUKE, O Lord, those who seek political results by taking to the streets, with banners and weapons, to threaten and intimidate. Persuade them that aggressive words and action do not solve problems or make peace.

Lord in your mercy
Hear our prayer

ENCOURAGE and strengthen, O Lord, those who are seeking ways and means of ensuring
> justice for criminals;
> shelter for the homeless;
> and a wholesome, happy life for the whole nation.

Lord in your mercy
Hear our prayer

O LORD Jesus Christ, who felt temptation's power but resisted it, help all who are seduced by perversion, or lured into fraud or theft, or enticed into the abuse of drugs or alcohol. Lead them away from temptation, we pray, and increase their resistance to evil.

Lord in your mercy
Hear our prayer

GIVE us, O Lord, the pity and determination to help in your name the aged and senile
> the incompetent and debt-ridden;
> the ill-housed and the homeless;
> and all who seek but cannot find work.

Lord in your mercy
Hear our prayer

HEAVENLY Father, into your loving hands we commend
> those who mourn a dear one departed;
> those soon to have a major operation;
> and those who are dying.

Father, into your hands.

Lord in your mercy
Hear our prayer

ETERNAL God, who sought and found us, and loves us today and for ever, we praise you for your saints, among whom
we remember especially those who taught us a bedtime
prayer, and told us the story of Jesus, and set us a Christian
example. When our time comes to die, may we be found
worthy to join them in glory, and rejoice together round your
heavenly throne; through Jesus Christ our Saviour, who lives,
loves and reigns with you, O Father, and the Holy Spirit, one
God, world without end.

Amen

THANKSGIVING

Sursum Corda

Minister:	Lift up your hearts
All:	*We lift them to the Lord*
Minister:	Let us give thanks to the Lord our God
All:	*It is right to give him thanks and praise*

Let us pray:

NOW on the heavenly altar we lay our sacrifice of thanksgiving to you, O Lord our God.

Worthy of all thanks and praise are you, our great and
loving Creator, who, from time immemorial, planned this
vast universe and in it a place for the human race.

Worthy of praise are you our heavenly Father, who, far

back in time, thought on us your children, brought us to life, sought our trust and love, arranged a costly salvation for us, and offered us an everlasting life.

As we remember your goodness, may we resolve to show our gratitude by obeying your will, doing the duties of love, and loyally serving the Church of Jesus Christ, to whom, with you O Father, and the Holy Spirit, be glory and honour throughout all ages.

Amen

9

GOD *is* LIGHT

HERE is the message we heard and pass on to you: that God is Light and in him there is no darkness at all.

Come let us walk in the light of the Lord.

Let us pray:

ALMIGHTY God, throned in splendour and surrounded with celestial light, mercifully regard us, creatures of darkness and half-lights, who dare to approach you.

As on the first morning of the world, you commanded light to appear, so may you now send a shaft of light into our minds, scattering the shadows of ignorance and error, doubt and sin; through Jesus Christ our Lord.

HOLY God, holy and mighty, holy and immortal, have mercy

upon us. The severity of your perfect light shows up the dark places in our thoughts and motives and lives. Forgive, O God, our wanton thoughts not banished immediately; our evil motives that lead us to do wrong; and our sadly selfish lives. Forgive, O Lord, the sins we remember, and also the sins which our conscience has forgotten, or hidden in our sub-conscious.

Lord have mercy
Christ have mercy
Lord have mercy

O GOD, whose nature is mercy and love, hear our humble confession. Forgive our sins. And cleanse us from the guilt and the memory of them; through the grace and power of your Son, our Saviour.

ALMIGHTY God, Lord of our lives, send us your light, we pray, to disperse the shadows cast by our doubts and fears.

LORD, without your light, we would go through life with faltering steps and slow, therefore shine on our path of duty.

LORD, that we may see more clearly your guiding light, remove the things which veil our eyes—pride, selfishness, and love of money.

LORD, we dread taking a new and unknown road, therefore strengthen our confidence in your light, even though it may lead through a black night of sorrow, or the dark door of death.

OUR FATHER ....

INTERCESSIONS

O GOD the Father, from whom the whole human family is named, hear our prayers for those who share with us your love and mercy.

FILL the Church, O God, in its many branches, with the splendour of the Gospel of Christ, which it exists to proclaim. Sweep away the shadows of sectarian prejudice, so that in charity we may all work together for the world's salvation, and the spread of your Kingdom.

Lord in your mercy
Hear our prayer

WE thank you, O God, that the Gospel can be preached in many lands without hindrance. May its bright light plunge into the darkest places of the earth, banishing superstition, abolishing slavery, and exposing the poverty of other faiths.

Lord in your mercy
Hear our prayer

SINCE a people perish where there is no vision, we pray you, Lord, to give insight to our legislators. Let neither power nor political dogma corrupt, or blind them. And may there appear in our nation a new respect for religion, a new morality, and a new joy in work.

Lord in your mercy
Hear our prayer

HEAVENLY Father, hear our prayer for those to whom your Son, our Saviour, gave particular care;

43

the sick and disabled;
the poor and disadvantaged;
and young children at risk from adults.
Look after them, O Lord. Make them aware of how fond you
are, and how near you are to help them.

Lord in your mercy
Hear our prayer

HEAR our prayer also, O Lord, for the tragic victims of drug
addiction, who bring misery on themselves and grief to their
parents. Plant in their heart a desire to reform, and a will to
be slaves no longer.

Lord in your mercy
Hear our prayer

O LORD Jesus Christ, seen by some as a light to the Gentiles
and a glory to your own people, fill the whole world with
your glory. And hasten the day when Jews and Gentiles will
sit down together in your Kingdom.

Lord in your mercy
Hear our prayer

ETERNAL God, while we praise you for your most famous
saints, who, row on row, surround your throne in glory, we
remember also countless plain folk, too humble to be named,
who loved the Lord Jesus Christ, some of whom turned our
faces to the light, and set our feet on the narrow way. May we
follow them in all good living, and meet them again in your
heaven; through Jesus Christ our Lord, to whom with you, O
Father, and the Holy Spirit, be given praise and honour, now
and to the end of the world.   *Amen*

THANKSGIVING

Sursum Corda

Minister:	Lift up your hearts
All:	*We lift them to the Lord*
Minister:	Let us give thanks to the Lord our God
All:	*It is right to give him thanks and praise*

Let us pray:

IT is indeed right to give thanks and praise to you, O God, the Light of the world, the brightness of innumerable holy lives, and the radiance that fills the courts of heaven.

WE praise you, O Lord, for the benefits and blessings given, without limit, to undeserving men and women; and, in particular, for
> the light of the majestic sun;
> the pale light of moon and stars;
> the light of human reason;
> the candle of conscience;
> and the torch of knowledge.

EVEN more we thank you, O Lord, for your Holy Word, which is a lamp to guide our feet, and a light on our path.

BUT most of all we praise you for your Son, our Saviour Jesus Christ, whose life is the light of mankind, which the darkness has never mastered.

BE pleased, O God, to accept our thanksgiving [along with these our offerings for the work of your Church]; through Jesus Christ our Lord, to whom with you and the Holy Spirit, be all praise and glory for ever.   *Amen*

10

GOD *is* LOVE

GOD is love; and his love was disclosed to us in this: that he sent his only Son into the world to bring us life.

If God thus loved us, dear friends, we in turn are bound to love one another.

Let us pray:

ALMIGHTY and everlasting God, with glad and grateful hearts we worship you, whose love embraces the whole human race, and continues, without change, the same, yesterday, today and tomorrow. We praise you for that love shown uniquely in the life and death of Jesus Christ, our Saviour. May the remembrance of his life make us eager to follow in his steps, and the memory of his death and resurrection keep us thankful for your love, and hopeful of an everlasting life.

OUR Father in heaven, your love surrounds us, like the very air we breathe. And yet we sometimes doubt your existence, and wonder if science has proved you are dead. Pardon our recurring fear that you are indifferent to human misery. Excuse our frequent complaints about the way you have ordered nature and planned human life.

Purge our souls, O God, of these thoughts. Drain our hearts of such bitter feelings. And forgive us our lack of a happy, childlike trust in your love;

Lord have mercy

Christ have mercy
Lord have mercy

REMEMBER how Jesus said: 'Take heart, my son; your sins are forgiven'. Remember and be comforted.

O GOD, whose love is so wide that, like the rain, it falls equally on the just and unjust, help us to love like you. Strengthen us, therefore, to rid ourselves of every form of prejudice so that we can love

> the poor as well as the rich;
> the simple as well as the clever;
> those like us and those very different;
> those who are kind, amusing, and easy to love;
> and those who are disagreeable, dull and rude;

help us for the sake of Jesus Christ our Lord.

HEAVENLY Father, whose providence includes the sparrows, and whose love provides food for the ravens, free us from the fear that you do not care what happens to us, and increase our confidence in your love—the love which, in Jesus Christ our Lord, reached out to save us.

OUR FATHER ....

INTERCESSIONS

O MERCIFUL God, as we start to pray for others, may we have complete confidence in your love and desire to help and heal and save.

WE pray for all who are suffering and feel forsaken by you; and for all who are crippled by disease, who feel unjustly treated by you.

47

O Lord, give them faith that you know them by name, and love each single person.

Lord in your mercy
Hear our prayer

WE pray for the neurotic, who know they are ill and long to be well; and for the melancholic, who have lost all hope of recovery.

O Lord, may they see evidence of your love in the kind treatment they receive.

Lord in your mercy
Hear our prayer

HEAVENLY Father, deal lovingly, we pray, with those recently bereaved; parents who have lost a child; children who have lost a parent; husbands and wives who have lost affection and respect for each other. Bless, O Lord, those unhappy people.

Lord in your mercy
Hear our prayer

FOR the Church, O God, we pray, that, filled with your Holy Spirit, it may persuade many to listen to the good news of your love, and lead many to discover in Christ their salvation in life, their comfort in sorrow, and their hope in death.

Lord in your mercy
Hear our prayer

ALMIGHTY God, we pray for peace in our warring world. Help us to remember that indifference to world peace is a

betrayal of Christ and his cause. Prompt us, therefore
    to think fairly,
    to love widely,
    and to speak without prejudice, and with courtesy.

> *Lord in your mercy*
> *Hear our prayer*

O LORD Jesus Christ, who knew the happiness of a home
in Nazareth, bless our homes. Care for any children there,
lest they come to harm; comfort any elderly persons under
our roof, that they may remain young in spirit.

> *Lord in your mercy*
> *Hear our prayer*

ALMIGHTY God, who in every age kindles the fire of your
love in the hearts of your saints, grant that we too may feel the
same warm love that produces good words and good deeds,
and fits us for everlasting life; through Jesus Christ our Lord,
to whom, with you, and the Holy Spirit, be glory and praise
world without end.   *Amen*

THANKSGIVING

Sursum Corda

Minister:	Lift up your hearts
All:	*We lift them to the Lord*
Minister:	Let us give thanks to the Lord our God
All:	*It is right to give him thanks and praise*

Let us pray:

ALMIGHTY God, we offer our thanks and praise to you the Creator of mankind by your love, and the generous provider of all things necessary to sustain and feed us.

Glory be to you, O Lord, for adding colour and design to your creation, which has increased our pleasure in living, and given us joy in looking on the sky and sea and countryside, and delight in watching the beauty of growing things.

Most of all we bless you, O Lord, for the wonder and glory of our immortal souls, which can respond to your love, and rejoice in the salvation won for us by your Son, our Saviour, Jesus Christ, who lives and loves and reigns with you and the Holy Spirit, one God, for ever and ever.

Amen

11

GOD *is* TRUTH

GOD is spirit, and those who worship him must worship in spirit and in truth.

Let us pray:

O GOD of truth, most wise, most great and most holy, in solemn reverence we bow before you. That we may worship you in spirit and in truth, clear our minds of pride and our hearts of self-love. Give us a childlike spirit that is eager to learn, and willing to be led by the hand; through Jesus Christ our Lord.

HEAVENLY Father, we have sinned and are not fit to be called your children. You are truth, but we have not always been truthful. Too often we have used speech to mislead and not inform other people. Too often we have used gestures and smiles to hide our thoughts and not reveal them. Too often we use words to hurt and not comfort. Forgive our deceit and our lies of tongue and pen.

Forgive also, O Lord, our failures to be truthful even with ourselves. Too often we have not admitted our faults. Too often we have persuaded ourselves that we are blameless. Forgive us those sins, and all other sins to which our conscience has now become blind.

Lord have mercy
Christ have mercy
Lord have mercy

MAY the Almighty and merciful Lord grant *us* forgiveness of *our* sins, time for amendment of life, and the grace and comfort of the Holy Spirit.   *Amen*

GIVE us, O God, an open mind lest we shut out a new truth, or a fresh insight revealed to us.

GIVE us, O God, open ears that we may listen to disagreeable truths, and obey your calls to duty without excuses.

GIVE us, O God, open eyes that we may never be blind to your presence, or fail to recognise goodness even in unlikely persons.

GIVE us, O God, open hearts that are not closed to the miseries of our fellow-creatures, but are always open to the touch of pity.

OUR FATHER ....

INTERCESSIONS

MOST merciful Father, touch our hearts with your pity for all your children, so that we may earnestly pray for other people in the name of Jesus Christ.

FOR the Church we pray, O Lord, the Church of the apostles and martyrs, the mother of our souls, now fallen here on evil days. Send your Holy Spirit in wind and fire to revive the Church and make it more able to win citizens for your Kingdom.

Lord in your mercy
Hear our prayer

FOR peace we pray, O Lord, for peace throughout this unhappy, quarrelling world. Spread a sense of brotherhood, like a contagious influence, among the nations that we may all live peaceably together.

Lord in your mercy
Hear our prayer

ALMIGHTY God, save our countrymen from ignoring the Christian Church, the bulwark of truth, and therefore lowering standards of conduct. Free us from dishonesty in trade, deceit in business, and fraud in professional life. And may none of us stoop to telling lies, or even being economical with the truth.

Lord in your mercy
Hear our prayer

LOVING Father, we pray for men and women in distress:
for anyone whose health, or heart is broken;
for anyone whose mind is diseased, or whose spirit is
troubled.

Lord in your mercy
Hear our prayer

DEAR heavenly Father, for the children of this generation
we pray, that they, being blessed with wise parents and good
teachers, may accumulate true information. And may they
also grow in the knowledge of your truth and your love.

Lord in your mercy
Hear our prayer

FATHER, into your hands we commend our loved ones and
our friends. And in silence we name those for whom we are,
at this time, anxious and concerned.

Lord in your mercy
Hear our prayer

WE honour your saints, O God. We thank you for eloquent
preachers of the Gospel; wise teachers of your truth; great
writers of poetry and prose; distinguished musicians and
artists.

Also we bless you for those men and women, undis-
tinguished by rank, or wealth, or talent, who in simplicity
loved you and their fellow men, and left behind an example
which reproves and rouses us. May we come at last to share
their joy in your heavenly Kingdom; through Jesus Christ
our Lord.

NOW to the King of both worlds, this and the next, to the immortal and invisible God, our Father in heaven, be honour and glory for ever.

Amen

THANKSGIVING

Sursum Corda

Minister:	Lift up your hearts
All:	*We lift them to the Lord*
Minister:	Let us give thanks to the Lord our God
All:	*It is right to give him thanks and praise*

Let us pray:

UNTO you, O God, we give thanks; unto you, the only true and living God, we give thanks for creating, sustaining, and developing mankind through unimaginable centuries.

We praise you for your patience with our slow growth in knowledge of the truth; with our long search for you through superstition, idolatry and paganism.

We bless you for the work of the Holy Spirit in good people in all ages and nations, but especially in the Hebrew prophets, who left us a great and partial revelation of your heart and mind.

Most of all, we praise you for the unique and perfect revelation embodied in Jesus Christ. By his light we see; by his teaching we learn your love; by his life we model our lives; by his death we die to sin; and by his resurrection we hope to be raised to heaven. And therefore, O God, our hearts bless you, our lips praise you, and our lives glorify you, now and evermore.

Amen

12

GOD *gives*

HEAR these words of our Lord Jesus Christ: 'Ask, and you will receive; seek, and you will find; knock, and the door will be opened'.

Let us pray:

ALMIGHTY God, heavenly Father, we worship you gladly and confidently. We know that you are more ready to give than we are to ask; more eager to be found than we are to seek; and more willing to open a door to new life or thought than we are to knock. Grant us grace, therefore, to ask for mercy, to seek for truth, and to knock on heaven's door; for the sake of Jesus Christ our Lord.

O GOD our merciful judge, we are ashamed to ask yet again for your pardon. But each one of us has a sorry tale to tell of sin and selfishness. Stop us from seeking excuses for our faults, or blaming our sins on our heredity or our surroundings. Prompt us instead to condemn ourselves for promising much, but doing little; for nursing good intentions, but allowing them to die; and for boasting of our talents, but not using them. Pardon these sins of omission, O Lord. Then mercifully pardon our sins of commission in words and deeds, which we deeply regret and confess with penitence.

> *Lord have mercy*
> *Christ have mercy*
> *Lord have mercy*

MAY the almighty and merciful Lord grant *you* pardon of all *your* sins, time for amendment of life, and the grace and comfort of the Holy Spirit.

Amen

HEAVENLY Father, to you we owe the precious gift of life, so we pray you to give us also the spirit to use the gift properly.

TEACH us, good Lord, to enjoy life in all seasons, and in every kind of weather, giving you thanks always for all things.

TEACH us, good Lord, to endure life with courage and a hopeful spirit, when there is pain to be borne, or a cross to be carried.

TEACH US, good Lord, teach us to accept life's discipline, and to perform life's duties without complaint, believing that some day all questions will be answered, all sorrows justified, and all good and faithful service praised.

OUR FATHER ....

INTERCESSIONS

ALMIGHTY God, heavenly Father, hear our humble prayers for men and women throughout the world who need your help.

In spite of the many differences of colour, race and nationality, may all people come to feel themselves members of your great family. Assure them that they are brothers and sisters who need study war no more.

Lord in your mercy
Hear our prayer

For our fellow-Christians, we pray that they and we may bear witness to the Faith in a convincing fashion,
> by our devotion to discipline and duty;
> by our charity to all and our good conduct;
> and by our obvious desire to follow Christ.

Lord in your mercy
Hear our prayer

O LORD Jesus Christ, who once sailed on the stormy sea of Galilee, regard with your favour all seafarers; the officers and men of the Royal Navy; members of our fishing-fleets; and those who man lifeboats or cross-channel ferries. Protect them from danger at sea, and give their families on land a firm trust in your love and care.

Lord in your mercy
Hear our prayer

O LORD Jesus Christ, once a carpenter and builder, teach all who labour with their hands and follow you in faith,
> to smite the rock;
> to lift the stone
> to cleave the wood;
and find you there, at the start of every day and every duty.

Lord in your mercy
Hear our prayer

O GOD of life and love, in your compassion come close to every sufferer. Comfort, in particular, our friends and acquaintances who are exposed to suffering and distress at this time.

> *Lord in your mercy*
> *Hear our prayer*

ETERNAL God, with thankful hearts we commemorate the saints, who asked for your help and were given it; who sought your guidance and found it; who knocked on your heart's door and saw it open wide in love. Unworthy though we are, may we be allowed to share the glory which they enjoy eternally with you, the Father, and the Son, and the Holy Spirit, one God, to whom be praise through time and eternity.

Amen

THANKSGIVING

Sursum Corda

Minister:	Lift up your hearts
All:	*We lift them to the Lord*
Minister:	Let us give thanks to the Lord our God
All:	*It is right to give him thanks and praise*

Let us pray:

O GOD, most merciful, kind and patient, to you we are indebted for this planet Earth, which you formed to be our home. We thank you for its beauty of mountain and moor, hill and valley, running water and restless sea, and for its trees and flowers and natural grass.

WE thank you too, O God, for the long development of the human body and mind; for the dawn of intelligence; for the feeling of reverence and the need to worship; and for the sense of right and wrong.

WE thank you more, O God our redeemer, for our deliverance from the power of evil and the chain of sin, which you planned and accomplished in the life, death and resurrection of Jesus Christ, your Son, our Saviour.

WE have received from you, O God, more than we asked or sought, and far more than we deserved. Therefore we offer you our thanks [and also our alms]; through Jesus Christ our Lord, to whom, with you and the Holy Spirit, be glory for evermore.

Amen

13

GOD *helps*

GOD himself has said, 'I will never leave you or desert you'; and so we can take courage and say, 'The Lord is my helper'.

Let us pray:

ALMIGHTY and everlasting God, you have been a safe refuge for our fathers, and a strong tower for your people in all generations; therefore we worship and praise you. On you we also rely for support; on you we depend for breath and bread; and to you we turn for the help we need, and are sure to receive, through the grace of our Lord and Saviour Jesus Christ.

MOST merciful God, humbly we confess to you that we are altogether unworthy of your mercy. You have given us innumerable and varied blessings, and we have received them as a matter of course. Given much, we have asked for more. Greatly blessed, we have been ungrateful. Greatly loved, we have been unloving. O Lord forgive our cold, indifferent hearts.

Forgive also, O Lord, our sins; the sins that are obvious to everyone, and the sins we hide from the world, but cannot hide from you.

> *Lord have mercy*
> *Christ have mercy*
> *Lord have mercy*

MAY God in his mercy forgive our sins, and grant us time to amend our lives with the strong help of the Holy Spirit.

ALMIGHTY God, having done so much for us already, we pray that you will do more. Grant us your help as we wrestle with our ancient enemies: the world, the flesh and the devil. Assist us also as we struggle forward on our earthly pilgrimage.

WHEN the road becomes steep and muddy; when our feet begin to slip;
> *Help us, O Lord.*

When we are tempted to stray and take the primrose path; when our conscience has nothing to say;

60

Help us, O Lord.

When resolution fails and hope is faint; when courage ebbs and faith goes with it;
> *Help us, O Lord.*

When old age is a burden to carry; when our journey's end comes in sight;
> *Help us, O Lord, we pray.*

OUR FATHER ....

INTERCESSIONS

MERCIFUL Father, since both duty and love insist that we pray for others in need, we ask you to hear us.

WAKEN, O Lord, in the hearts of Christian believers a longing to see the world entirely at peace, and all the nations working together. To that end may your Holy Spirit persuade opponents that discussion is better than fighting, and forgiveness is better than taking revenge.

> *Lord in your mercy*
> *Hear our prayer*

O GOD, whose Son taught us that whatever good we do for others is done for you, grant us grace to act always with love and generosity. When offered the chance may we
>   satisfy the needs of the hungry;
>   befriend the stranger;
>   nurse the sick;
>   and visit those in prison.

Lord in your mercy
Hear our prayer

HEAVENLY Father, who created us with fragile bodies, we ask you to bless all who try to prevent disease, or cure sickness, or mend limbs, or lessen the burdens of old age. Encourage them with the thought that they work with the great Physician himself, our Saviour Jesus Christ.

Lord in your mercy
Hear our prayer

GIVE wisdom and ability, O Lord, to the men and women who govern us, make our laws, and order justice. Infuse with a kindly spirit all those in the caring professions, that they may be gentle with those who want information, or, having fallen on hard times, need assistance.

Lord in your mercy
Hear our prayer

LORD Jesus Christ, who lifted little children into your arms and blessed them, we pray for those persons who deal with small children; all fathers, mothers, and relatives; all teachers in Sunday Schools, or Primary Schools. Bless them with the affection and understanding you felt for children.

Lord in your mercy
Hear our prayer

ALL honour and praise be given to you, the everlasting God, for your many saints, who, row on row, surround your throne in glory. Their memory is treasured by us; their example is a constant inspiration to us. Forbid it, O Lord, that we should fall from grace while watched by these great souls, or be denied entrance to that place prepared for all your good and faithful servants.

NOW to you, Father, Son and Holy Spirit, the divine and undivided Trinity, be all praise, world without end.

Amen

THANKSGIVING

Sursum Corda

Minister:	Lift up your hearts
All:	*We lift them to the Lord*
Minister:	Let us give thanks to the Lord our God
All:	*It is right to give him thanks and praise*

Let us pray:

GLADLY we give you thanks, O God, our heavenly Father, because from our quiet homes and first beginnings you loved us, guarded and guided us, saved us by your son Jesus Christ, and sheltered us in his Church.

WE thank you also for our life here in our native land, a land which for many centuries has heard the sound of a church-going bell, listened to the preaching of the Gospel, and responded to your praise in holy psalms.

LAY it ever on our memories, O Lord, that much will be required of us, to whom so much has been given. And, therefore [as we dedicate this offering to the work of the

Church], we promise to support your cause to the best of our ability; through Jesus Christ our Lord.

NOW unto the God of all grace, who called us into his eternal glory by Christ Jesus, be glory and dominion for ever and ever.

Amen

14

GOD *commands*

THE Lord's love never fails those ... who listen to his voice ... who remember his commandments and obey them.

Let us pray:

ALMIGHTY and eternal God, who sits upon the heavenly throne, at whose command the universe was formed and light appeared, we bow before you in awe and adoration.

With the whole company of your people on earth and in heaven, we join in praising you for all that you have done and for all that you are; through Jesus Christ our Lord.

O GOD most high and holy, we acknowledge that in ancient times you gave your commandments to mankind. We have tried to keep them, but have failed. We have heard your voice, but paid little attention. We have seen the path of duty, but have not followed it. We have done wrong many times and in many ways and are deeply sorry for our sins. Our hearts condemn us, but with you, O Lord, pity and pardon can be found.

Lord have mercy
Christ have mercy
Lord have mercy

MAY our merciful God forgive all our sins, free us from them entirely, and raise us to new life in Jesus Christ.

ALMIGHTY God, who established the Ten Commandments as a moral standard for all mankind, incline our hearts to keep your law.
   We therefore pray, O Lord,
      that we may banish from our minds any idol or super-stition, and reverence you alone, our God and redeemer.
   And we pray, O Lord,
      that we may keep Sunday as a memorial of our Lord's resurrection, and use it for the re-creation of body and soul.
   And we pray, O Lord,
      that we may honour our parents, respect every living creature, and keep married life pure and happy.
   And we pray, O Lord,
      that we may never lay hands on what is not ours, nor tell lies, nor speak ill of our neighbours, nor covet the possessions of other people.
Grant this, O Lord, for the sake of Jesus Christ our Saviour.

OUR FATHER ....

INTERCESSIONS

HEAVENLY Father, hear our prayers for the Church and the world.

STRENGTHEN the Church, O Lord, in its service of your Kingdom. Enable it to gather in the lost of this generation, by presenting the Person of Jesus, who in Galilee spoke to people who knew him not, the word of command: 'Follow me'.

Lord in your mercy
Hear our prayer

REGARD, O God, with special concern, the prophet-people of Israel, so long prepared to hail the coming of the Messiah. Let not their destiny be further delayed. May they find at last all their great hopes and dreams fulfilled in your Son Jesus Christ.

Lord in your mercy
Hear our prayer

FATHER of us all, we pray for criminals who have broken your commandments and the laws of our country and suffer now in prison. Bring them to repentance. We pray also for all scoundrels and fraudsters who are at liberty, but should be in jail. Confront them with the Ten Commandments. Stab their consciences into active life with some sacred memory.

Lord in your mercy
Hear our prayer

WITH compassion, O God, we remember the struggling poor, mothers who must bring up children on their own; workers who have been made redundant, and those so greatly handicapped that employment is impossible. May they have adequate nutrition and housing, and be given the assurance that you care what happens to them.

Lord in your mercy
Hear our prayer

REPROACH, O Lord, the self-satisfied and smugly pious, who obey the letter of every law, but abuse and condemn their brothers and sisters who offend. Teach them that love alone fulfills the law of Christ—and that they can only approach God with confidence if they keep his commands and do what he approves.

Lord in your mercy
Hear our prayer

TO your great kindness, O God, we commend people who at present are sick and in pain; those who are afraid of a necessary operation; those who have to depend on strangers for daily help; and those who see with dread their journey's end approaching.

Lord in your mercy
Hear our prayer

EVERLASTING God, we rejoice in the memory of your faithful servants in every age, whose shining goodness rebuked a sinful world. Gaining courage from their example, may we persevere in our pilgrimage, walking forward confidently to the holy city new Jerusalem, where we hope to join the saints in praising you our God, Father, Son and Holy Spirit blessed for ever and ever.

Amen

THANKSGIVING

Sursum Corda

Minister: Lift up your hearts
All: *We lift them to the Lord*
Minister: Let us give thanks to the Lord our God
All: *It is right to give him thanks and praise*

Let us pray:

MERCIFUL God, generous Father in heaven, we thank and praise you, because you have done so much for us, and most of it unnoticed; and because you have given us so much, and all of it undeserved. Greatly indebted to you as we are, we pray for one more gift—a grateful heart.

O LORD Jesus Christ, we thank you because you came down to earth and suffered here for our sake, guiding us by your words, inspiring us by your deeds, redeeming us by your death on the Cross, and giving us hope of an eternal life by your resurrection.

O HOLY Spirit, we thank you because you cleanse our thoughts and revive our spirits, and because you rebuke human sin, raise moral standards, and give light and life to the Church.

THEREFORE to you O God, Father, Son and Holy Spirit, one great and blessed Trinity, we give our thanks and praise, now and evermore.

Amen

15

WORSHIP *of* GOD

THE BIDDING

WE have come together in the presence of Almighty God to offer him our worship and praise; to make confession of our sins; and to pray both for ourselves and others. Wherefore let us be seated, and remember God's presence with us now.

O GOD, almighty, immortal, invisible, we worship you. Although we cannot see you, we are aware of your presence. Although we are sinful, we realise your holiness. Therefore subdue our spirits with a sense of your immeasurable power and perfection, so that we come before you in reverence and humility; through Jesus Christ our Lord.

HOLY and transcendent God, we hand ourselves over to your mercy, for we are wayward, foolish and sinful creatures, and have much to confess to you. Forgive us, O Lord. O Lord forgive us our sins, the sins of our youth, and our present sins, sins which are manifest to all the world, and sins which we have so laboured to hide from the world, that now they are hid from our own conscience. O Lord forgive even our worship, which often has been cold and formal, our praise lifeless, and our prayers insincere. Cover our faults with your love, which sees all, hears all, knows all, and yet is willing to pardon all.

Lord have mercy
Christ have mercy
Lord have mercy

MAY the almighty and merciful Lord grant unto *you* pardon and remission of all *your* sins, time for amendment of life, and the grace and comfort of the Holy Spirit.

O LORD Jesus Christ, who made it your custom to attend a house of God for public worship on the day appointed, persuade us to acquire this habit and go to church regularly, keeping one day in the week holy.

O LORD Jesus Christ, who rejected the temptation to gain a world-wide dominion by employing the devil's methods, restrain us from ever using dishonourable means to win worldly success.

O LORD Jesus Christ, who warned us that we cannot serve both God and Money, remind us of this repeatedly, lest we pay homage to God with our lips, but in our hearts worship wealth and worldly goods.

OUR FATHER ....

INTERCESSIONS

MERCIFUL God and heavenly Father, we bear on our hearts

the great number of persons who are troubled in body or mind or spirit.

WE pray first for the Church as it struggles with the desertion of many members, the disloyalty of others, and the disinterest of the general public. May the Church seek fresh inspiration from worship; may it find new enthusiasm from praise; may it gain new hope from prayer.

Lord in your mercy
Hear our prayer

LOVING Father, to whom all your children are dear: Jew and Gentile, Hindu and Buddhist, Moslem and Christian. Remind us that we are all members of your worshipping family. Melt hard prejudices; warm cold hearts; and bend stubborn wills, through the reconciling power of your Holy Spirit.

Lord in your mercy
Hear our prayer

O GOD of all life, whose concern for your humble creatures includes even the fall of a sparrow, we pray that no one will use cruelty on birds, or on any animal, wild or domesticated, but will treat these unoffending fellow-creatures with respect and affection.

Lord in your mercy
Hear our prayer

HEAVENLY Father, whose Son once fed a hungry crowd with loaves and fishes, we pray for those who suffer from hunger through lack of bread, because of natural disaster or

71

the greed of mankind. Prosper the labours of those who try to provide the starving with food and fuel, wells for water and seeds for crops. Bless also the work of those ministers of religion who take to those unfortunates the bread of life, so that they may never hunger in spirit.

Lord in your mercy
Hear our prayer

O LORD, invisible but ever-present, grant that your servants here, whether they travel on holiday or on business, may remember that they are not exempt from prayer and worship, but can find you near to them day and night.

Lord in your mercy
Hear our prayer

FATHER in heaven, from whom we came at our beginning, and to whom we shall go at our end, we praise you for those who have gone before us; the good, brave and unselfish men and women who worshipped you here on earth, and did your holy will. May our memory of them never fade, but remain a kindly rebuke and a powerful inspiration; through Jesus Christ our Lord.

NOW unto the God of all grace, who has called us to his eternal glory by Christ Jesus, be glory and dominion for ever and ever.

Amen

THANKSGIVING

Sursum Corda

Minister:	Lift up your hearts
All:	*We lift them to the Lord*
Minister:	Let us give thanks to the Lord our God
All:	*It is right to give him thanks and praise*

Let us pray:

WE give praise and thanks to you, heavenly Father, for your presence which moves our hearts to worship, and fills them with contentment and peace.

Glory to you, O God, for ever.

WE thank you, almighty Lord, because you created the world and everything in it, and provided food and fruits, plants and flowers for us to enjoy.

Glory to you, O God, for ever.

WE thank you, Father, most of all for the revelation of your love and mercy in Jesus Christ; for the costly salvation he won for us on Calvary's Cross; and for his Church to take care of our souls, until we come to the end of this mortal life and the beginning of an everlasting life.

Glory to you, O God, for ever and ever.

Amen

Part II
SERVICES *for* SEASONS *of the* CHRISTIAN YEAR

1

FIRST SUNDAY *in* ADVENT

THE BIDDING

ADVENT is a Season, comprising the four Sundays before Christmas. This Season brings into view the preparation for our Lord's coming by the Law and the Prophets, and by his forerunner, John the Baptist.

Let us pray:

GLORY be to you, Almighty and Everlasting God. We praise you, because at the world's creation, when there was darkness everywhere, you commanded light to appear. And, when the human race was in the dark, you sent your Son Jesus Christ, whose life is the light of mankind.

Prepare a way, O Lord, for his coming at this time. Make ready our hearts to receive him. And grant us grace to welcome his appearing.

O HOLY God, in your light we all live, although many prefer darkness. We who walk in your light are ashamed that you should see us as we are, for the light exposes hands that are unclean, hearts that are impure, and motives that are black. We confess also that there are certain deeds and plans which we keep hidden from others, but are all seen by you. Father, we beg you to forgive us, for the sake of our Saviour Jesus Christ.

Lord have mercy
Christ have mercy
Lord have mercy

MAY our merciful God pardon your sins; strengthen you in all goodness; and grant you everlasting life; through Jesus Christ our Lord.

ALMIGHTY God, who prepared for the first coming of Jesus Christ to our world by the preaching of John the Baptist and his call to repentance, prepare our nation to celebrate the birth of our Lord. Rebuke all sinners; reprove the worldly; restore the penitent. Deliver us from our faults and remove from our minds the attraction of wickedness, replacing it with a genuine love of goodness. Thus shall we be made ready to go to Bethlehem in imagination, and worship the Holy Child.

O LORD Jesus Christ, your Church has long been waiting for your coming again to the world. May we continue to watch and hope for the final victory of your Kingdom, when you come in glory at the last day.

OUR FATHER ....

INTERCESSIONS

HEAVENLY Father, our loving guardian and helper, first in our prayers of concern must come the Church of Jesus Christ.

WE pray that the Church, envigorated by the Holy Spirit, may preach boldly the Gospel, and fearlessly condemn racial hatred, political violence, and every form of oppression. Give persuasive power to the Church as it insists that all men and women are brothers and sisters, belong to one family, have you as their Father, and Christ as their Saviour.

Lord in your mercy
Hear our prayer

FOR the world, we pray, that a brotherly spirit may enjoy such an advent that old resentments are removed, old grudges forgotten, and a new period of peace is begun. Thus may the song of angels at Bethlehem be realised: 'Glory to God in the highest, and on earth peace, goodwill among men'.

Lord in your mercy
Hear our prayer

O LORD, we pray for the people who at this holiday season will travel on roads that are busy, or in the air during bad weather. Send your Holy Spirit to caution all travellers, so that they do not put at risk their own lives, or the lives of others.

Lord in your mercy
Hear our prayer

HEAR our prayer, O God, for doctors, surgeons and nurses, and for ambulance crews, who attend patients critically ill, injured or dying. Raise their spirits with the assurance that what they do compassionately for other men and women, they do for you.

Lord in your mercy
Hear our prayer

O LORD Jesus Christ, for whose first coming here no better room than a stable was found, be near to those who sleep rough in our cities, and all whose dwellings are squalid, damp and dirty. Speak to them of your concern, and arouse the community to meet their need.

Lord in your mercy
Hear our prayer

GUARD and guide us, Almighty God, throughout our earthly pilgrimage, be it short or long, in calm or stormy weather. And keep us remembering your saints and all the good and faithful people who have gone before us to heaven's gate, because their fellowship shall be such a help to us 'as wings are to a bird, or sails are to a ship'.

NOW unto the God of all grace, who has called us to his eternal glory by Christ Jesus, be glory and dominion for ever and ever.

Amen

THANKSGIVING

Sursum Corda

Minister:	Lift up your hearts
All:	*We lift them to the Lord*
Minister:	Let us give thanks to the Lord our God
All:	*It is right to give him thanks and praise*

Let us pray:

MERCIFUL God, heavenly Father, infinitely great, wise and

good, we worship you, praising you

for your power which made and sustains all people
and things;

for your wisdom which governs the spinning planets,
and the whole world of nature;

and for your love which arranged a costly salvation for
us in the person of Jesus Christ.

GLORY to you, O God, for Christ's coming as a little child, speechless as any baby, yet the eternal Word made flesh; born in a stable, yet the Prince of glory. We thank you for his adult life as a carpenter, yet the supreme Teacher; a victim of man's inhumanity, yet the Saviour of mankind.

FOR your great mercy to us, and for your love to all men and women everywhere, we praise your holy Name, world without end.

Amen

2

SECOND SUNDAY *in* ADVENT

[THEME: The Holy Bible]

THE Word of God is alive and active. It cuts more keenly than any two-edged sword .... It sifts the purpose and thoughts of the heart.

Let us pray:

ETERNAL God, the Word, the Truth, the Living Lord, prepare our hearts to worship you with proper reverence. Speak to us through our prayers and hymns of praise, and through the reading and preaching of your holy Word. Speak, Lord, to your servants, for we are listening.

ALMIGHTY Lord, we who are your unruly and disobedient servants, confess our many faults and humbly seek your forgiveness. We have turned a deaf ear to your commandments. We have rejected the reproof of the prophets. We have ignored the advice of the apostles. And, although long acquainted with the teaching of Christ, we still do not practice it as we ought to do. Father, we have sinned in your sight, and condemn ourselves for our weak will, our slumbering conscience, and our stupid confidence in our own virtue.

> *Lord have mercy*
> *Christ have mercy*
> *Lord have mercy*

MAY our merciful God grant us forgiveness of our sins, the will to amend our lives, and the Holy Spirit to help us resist our temptations and keep the commandments.

O HOLY Spirit, enable us to keep all these commandments:
>   to worship God alone and no other;
>   to reverence the sabbath and our parents too;
>   to discipline our strongest passions;
>   to indulge in no falsehood;
>   and to banish every covetous thought.

ALMIGHTY God, who gave us the Bible as a rule for life,

and the unique revelation of your great love for the human race, and your will and power to save it, grant that we may always cherish this holy Book. Help us to read and study it with care, and ever value its message of salvation through your Son, our Saviour Jesus Christ.

OUR FATHER ....

INTERCESSIONS

HEAR us, O heavenly Father, as we pray for others in the name of Jesus Christ.

FOR all members of the human race we pray, and for the universal Church of Christ, the messenger to them of your love and merciful offer of salvation.

Give the Church, we pray, a wider and more effective appeal, so that the Gospel it preaches may be hailed as good news for today, and its fellowship accepted as the pattern for a world community.

Lord in your mercy
Hear our prayer

ALMIGHTY God, our hearts are burdened with the thought of millions of men and women who have not heard the Gospel message, or read about the Saviour's life and death. May Bible Societies be well supported by the public, and receive your richest blessing. Direct the good seed of the Scriptures on to fertile ground, so that a great harvest of souls may be gathered in.

Lord in your mercy

Hear our prayer

GOD of pity and love, we remember also the millions of people with sick bodies, or sore hearts, or troubled souls. We earnestly pray that
    the diseased are given a remedy;
    the invalids return to health;
    the sorrowful are comforted;
    the despondent are invigorated.
And, O Shepherd of souls, be a shepherd to the dying, who will fear no evil, if you are with them through the valley of death.

Lord in your mercy
Hear our prayer

HEAVENLY Father, we pray for those who have fallen among thieves and been injured. May there be many good samaritans on the road who will stop and give help. And we pray for those who have left home and recklessly fallen from grace. May there be fathers ready to welcome the repentant prodigals home, in the name of Jesus Christ.

Lord in your mercy
Hear our prayer

BLESS this kingdom, O Lord. Deliver its citizens from worldliness, indulgence and vice. Enable the forces of law and order to protect the public, punish the wicked, and deal with the cruel and corrupted. Thus may we become a people ruled according to your Word, living in godliness and peace.

Lord in your mercy
Hear our prayer

O GOD of our salvation, keep us ever in fellowship with the
faithful departed, with psalmists and prophets, apostles,
saints and martyrs, preachers and evangelists. Were we to
travel always in their company, we could not fail to arrive
safely in heaven, where you the Father, and the Son, and the
Holy Spirit live and reign, one God for ever and ever.

Amen

THANKSGIVING

Sursum Corda

Minister:	Lift up your hearts
All:	*We lift them to the Lord*
Minister:	Let us give thanks to the Lord our God
All:	*It is right to give him thanks and praise*

Let us pray:

IT is both a duty and a joy to praise you, most gracious and
generous God. You have given us gifts and benefits innumerable, not the least of which is the Holy Bible—'the
most valuable thing this world affords'. We thank you for
the Bible's history of your dealing with your ancient,
chosen people, whose lives were sweetened by the hope
of a Messiah.

Especially at this season, we thank you for the evangelist's
story of the birth of Jesus at Bethlehem, and the account of
his life, death and resurrection. We rejoice to read that he
healed bodies and souls: not of Jews only, but of Gentiles;
not of the rich only, but of the poor; not of the privileged
only, but of the humble; not of men only, but of women; and
not of the pious only, but of sinners also.

85

AND therefore to Jesus the Messiah, the Word made flesh, the Prince of Peace, our Saviour, with you the Father and the Holy Spirit, we give thanks and praise for ever.

Amen

3

CHRISTMAS

THE angel said: 'Behold, I bring you good news of a great joy which will come to all people; for to you is born this day in the city of David a Saviour, who is Christ the Lord'.

(Luke 2:10-11, *Revised Standard Version*)

Let us pray:

YOU are worthy of all praise, O Lord our God, heavenly Father, for sending your Son to dwell among us. We thank you for the Holy Child born in Bethlehem, who came down from highest heaven to rescue a fallen world, and reveal to all your love and mercy.

MAY our celebration of his birth provide gladness for young and old, to our great good and your greater glory; through Jesus Christ our Lord.

HOLY and compassionate God, we are humbled to remember that your son was born not in power, but in weakness, not in pomp but in simplicity, not in a palace but in a stable. The manner of his coming makes us ashamed of our love of display, our delight in money, and our greed for more of everything. Forgive, O Lord, the importance we attach to wealth, and the honour we pay to people with rank, or great possessions. Forgive also, the scorn we sometimes feel for the poor, the thriftless and unemployed.

Lord have mercy
Christ have mercy
Lord have mercy

ALMIGHTY God have mercy on *us*; pardon and deliver *us* from all *our* sins; confirm and strengthen *us* in all goodness; and bring *us* to everlasting life; through Jesus Christ our Lord.

Amen

O LORD Jesus Christ, you chose to be born among us and be the friend and saviour of sinners, may we now choose to have you born again in our hearts through faith.

O LORD Jesus Christ, you were given once the mean reception of a stable; may the Holy Spirit sweep and scour our unclean hearts and make them fit to receive you.

O LORD Jesus Christ, for whose birth in Bethlehem no proper place was found, we pray that you will be formed within our hearts at this time, and accept from us, instead of myrrh, our penitence; instead of incense, our reverence; and instead of gold, our most precious gift—our love.

OUR FATHER ....

INTERCESSIONS

MOST merciful God, who makes us glad each year with the remembrance of the birth of Jesus Christ, we pray for those who are not happy this Christmastide.

GRACIOUS God, as the whole Church celebrates at this time, we pray that joy will smother the jealousies and dissensions that exist among us. Help us to act together in the huge task of taking the Gospel to all people and bringing all people to you.

> *Lord in your mercy*
> *Hear our prayer*

TO your pity and care, O God, we commend all who are confined to hospital beds through disease or accident. May the joyful message of this season lift their spirits and speed their recovery.

> *Lord in your mercy*
> *Hear our prayer*

SEND your Holy Spirit, O God, to soften the hearts of the many men and women justly imprisoned for their crimes. May the innocence of the Holy Child of Bethlehem remind them of their own early innocence, and fill them with regret, and a deep desire for reform.

> *Lord in your mercy*
> *Hear our prayer*

O GOD, mankind's judge and king, rebuke and condemn those who break the peace. Give every nation a spirit of brotherhood, and a willingness to act together against aggressors. Make peace, Lord, between Arabs and Jews, whites and blacks, men and women, parents and children, through the teaching and example of Christ, the Prince of Peace.

Lord in your mercy
Hear our prayer

HEAVENLY Father, as our thoughts are on the Child of Bethlehem, we pray earnestly for all infants and children. May they be treated always with patience, understanding and affection. And may the homes of our country at this season be places where goodwill and joy abound. This we ask for Jesus' sake.

Lord in your mercy
Hear our prayer

O LORD of life and death, with thanksgiving we remember your saints; the prophets who prepared the way for Christ's coming; the priests who taught people to pray and sing your praise; the disciples who supported our Lord in Galilee, and then took his Gospel to the world. We also remember and thank you for those dear to us, who took us to church, told us the story of Jesus, set us a good example, and shared with us the joy of Christmas. Mercifully grant that, after crossing the river of death, we may meet them again on that beautiful farther shore; through Jesus Christ our Saviour.

UNTO him that loved us, and washed us from our sins in his own blood, who has made us kings and priests unto God; to him be glory and dominion, for ever and ever.

Amen

THANKSGIVING

Sursum Corda

Minister:	Lift up your hearts
All:	*We lift them to the Lord*
Minister:	Let us give thanks to the Lord our God
All:	*It is right to give him thanks and praise*

Let us pray:

BLESSING, and glory, and thanksgiving be unto you our God, the Father of our Lord Jesus Christ, for sending your Son to a world damaged by sin and infected by evil. We thank you that

> when the need was greatest;
> when the time had come;
> when people looked and longed for a deliverer,
> then Christ came to the rescue.

HEAVENLY Father, we celebrate with joy at this time his humble, human birth; his childhood fed on holy psalms and prophesies; his faithful toil at a carpenter's bench; his blessed ministry of healing and preaching; and his saving death upon the Cross.

WITH all our heart we bless you, O God, for your innumerable blessings, but chiefly for Jesus Christ our Saviour, your greatest gift to undeserving men and women. Therefore with one accord, and with one voice, we glorify you, our God, the Father of our Lord Jesus Christ.

Amen

4

PALM SUNDAY

INTRODUCTION

ON this day our Lord rode into Jerusalem and was greeted by cheering crowds waving palm branches. They shouted: 'Blessings on him who comes in the name of the Lord! Hosanna in the heavens!'

Let us pray:

ALMIGHTY and everlasting God, we worship and praise you for sending your Son Jesus Christ to share our human life, and save our human nature. And, as today we celebrate our Lord's entry into Jerusalem, amidst a cheering crowd waving palm branches, may the scene epitomise for us his final glorious triumph, when every knee shall bow, and every tongue confess him King of glory.

O HOLY Father, we are ashamed that your son came in love to rescue sinners, but received injustice and ill-treatment and was cruelly put to death. And we are grieved to see Christ crucified afresh in the crimes and cruelties of our society. Many act as his Caiaphas by disregarding the claims of justice and religion. Many act as his Pontius Pilate by washing their hands of moral responsibility. Others act as his Judas by betraying his cause. And we who have claimed to be his disciples, have run away at a crucial moment. We have raised our voices in loud hosannas, but have not raised our hands to help him. Sore at heart and humble, we come to you for pardon.

Lord have mercy
Christ have mercy
Lord have mercy

JESUS said: 'Take heart, my son; your sins are forgiven'.

O LORD our God, help us to understand that your Son died to save us from sin, not from suffering. Teach us, therefore, that the hosannas of the crowd are not to be valued, and may turn to cries of hate. Teach us, too, that keeping to the path of duty could lead to a cross and not to a throne. Teach us, also, that doing your will faithfully could result in a crown of thorns and not a chaplet of roses. Teach us, Lord, how to live.

OUR FATHER ....

INTERCESSIONS

MOST merciful God, help us now to think beyond this place of human beings in need of you, and of the wide world in need of committed Christians.

BLESS abundantly, O Lord, all believing people who on this Palm Sunday are worshipping Christ the King and Saviour. May they find joy in exalting him as the redeemer of all mankind, proclaiming his Gospel of love in a loveless world.

Lord in your mercy
Hear our prayer

O GOD, whose son was born amongst the Jews, and reared in their traditions, look favourably on that ancient race at whose feet we have learned to pray. Open their eyes to see in Jesus their long expected Messiah; open their hearts to receive him as Saviour.

Lord in your mercy
Hear our prayer

O GOD, whose Son refused to be moved by the clamour of a crowd, we pray you to raise up honourable men and women of integrity to rule and lead our nation. Let not the shouts of the mob, or abuse from opponents, deflect them from doing what they judge to be right.

Lord in your mercy
Hear our prayer

O GOD, whose Son saved the soul of a robber on Calvary, rouse the conscience and soften the heart of imprisoned criminals. Bring them to repentance, and summon helpers to aid their reformation.

Lord in your mercy
Hear our prayer

LOVING Father, we remember and sympathise with those who will have little joy on this holy day. We beg you to help them.

Ease the distress of the sick and suffering.
Comfort everyone who mourns the loss of a dear one.
Protect and provide for deserted wives, and widows and orphaned children.
Befriend the lonely, the housebound and the aged.
And on the brow of the dying, lay your hand to comfort and bless.

93

Lord in your mercy
Hear our prayer

WE praise you, O God, for your saints, whose fellowship we enjoy as we journey through life. In particular we thank you for many good Christian people we have loved and lost and hope to meet again; those saints whose faces averted from us in sadness, or disgust, would be more than we could bear. Strengthen us, therefore, to follow Christ as they did, so that we may arrive unashamed at our journey's end.

AND now to you O God, Father, Son and Holy Spirit, be all honour and glory throughout all ages.

Amen

THANKSGIVING

Sursum Corda

Minister:	Lift up your hearts
All:	*We lift them to the Lord*
Minister:	Let us give thanks to the Lord our God
All:	*It is right to give him thanks and praise*

Let us pray:

O GOD, our heavenly Father, we gladly join this day with the whole Church on earth in worshipping you with loud hosannas, and singing the praise of Jesus Christ your Son, our Lord and King.

WE bless and thank you for the birth of Jesus in Bethlehem, fulfilling the hopes and dreams of the devout in many ages; for his life of patient labour as a craftsman in Nazareth; for

94

his ministry of healing and teaching in Galilee; for his claim on Palm Sunday to be the promised Messiah and expected King; for his death on the Cross, offering salvation from sin; and for his glorious resurrection, confirming all that he said and did.

ALL things are ours, thanks be to God! All things are ours in life or in death, in the present or in time to come, and all through Jesus Christ our Lord.

PRAISE and glory and wisdom, thanksgiving and honour, power and might, be to our God for ever and ever.

Amen

5

GOOD FRIDAY

INTRODUCTION

ON this day our Lord was tried, scourged, mocked and condemned to death.

> He was led to Calvary and, at nine o'clock, was nailed to the cross, crucified between two criminals.
> From then onward He suffered pain, thirst and desolation.
> And at three o'clock He bowed his head and died.

Let us pray:

ASSIST us mercifully with your help, O Lord God of our Salvation, that we may approach with reverence to the meditation of this mighty act whereby you have given us life and immortality; through Jesus Christ our Lord.

(The Crucifixion: *John 19:13-27; Mark 15:1-41*)

Let us pray:

ALMIGHTY and merciful God, we praise you that Jesus Christ came down to this fallen world to save sinners like us. We thank you that, in order to rescue and redeem us, he endured the deceitfulness of human minds, the evil of human hearts, and the cruelty of human hands, and died, forgiving all, upon the Cross.

Keep his Cross and conflict in our remembrance, that we also may try to overcome hatred with love, and evil with good, and violence with forgiveness, in the name and spirit of our Lord Jesus Christ.

O HOLY God, with shame we acknowledge that minds like ours planned Christ's death; that hearts like ours caused him to suffer; that hands like ours nailed him to the cross. He was wounded for our transgressions. He was bruised for our iniquities. And therefore we detest our sins, and sincerely repent of them.

> *Lord have mercy*
> *Christ have mercy*
> *Lord have mercy*

ALMIGHTY God, once more show us your mercy and wash away our guilt, casting all our sins into the depths of the sea; for the sake of Jesus Christ our Saviour.

O LORD Jesus Christ, carpenter of Nazareth, from the wood and nails of the cross you have constructed a crutch for our souls. Grant us grace to use that crutch to support us, until we reach the end of our pilgrimage.

O LORD Jesus Christ, who on this day suffered and died for us all, may your wounds heal us, and your death give us life everlasting.

OUR FATHER . . . .

THANKSGIVING

Sursum Corda

Minister:	Lift up your hearts
All:	*We lift them to the Lord*
Minister:	Let us give thanks to the Lord our God
All:	*It is right to give him thanks and praise*

Let us pray:

MERCIFUL God, the creator, preserver and redeemer of the human race, never more than on this particular and holy day do we praise and bless you for your Son our Saviour Jesus Christ.

WE remember today with shame how Jesus was falsely accused by priests and religious leaders, condemned by unjust judges, insulted by soldiers, deserted by his own disciples, abandoned by people to whom he had given health and sanity, sight and hearing, and finally marched by his executioners to a cruel death on the cross.

WE remember with thanksgiving the sacrifice Christ made on the cross, and we repeat the words of John: 'To him who loves us and freed us from our sins with his life's blood—to him be glory and dominion for ever and ever!'

Amen

INTERCESSION

Let us pray:

ALMIGHTY God, Father of our Lord Jesus Christ, on this day when the Church remembers especially the crucifixion of its King and Head, we pray you to grant its committed members a fresh flood of spiritual life, and a new determination to extend his Kingdom.

Lord in your mercy
Hear our prayer

WE pray for our contemporaries, who turn a deaf ear to the Gospel, and a blind eye to the Cross of Christ. Send your Holy Spirit to break the crust of their disinterest, and convince them that Christ could give their lives deeper meaning and greater satisfaction.

Lord in your mercy
Hear our prayer

WE pray, O God, for those who carry a cross of pain; for men and women who are diseased or disabled, who are burdened with fear or grief. Assure them that you care and are willing to help them carry their cross.

Lord in your mercy
Hear our prayer

WE pray for your ancient people the Jews, whose forefathers brought about the death of Jesus. Because we both have much in common and share your love and pity, may they be united with us in one family of Christian faith.

Lord in your mercy
Hear our prayer

WE pray, O God, for all persons troubled by the thought of death:
    for those suffering from a fatal disease;
    for those who are aged and growing weaker;
    and for those who live in fear of what is to come.
May they cling to Christ and trust in him, and confidently say, as he did: 'Father, into your hands I commit my spirit'.

Lord in your mercy
Hear our prayer

HEAVENLY Father, gently lead all dying believers through the dark door into that heavenly home prepared for them. May they fear nothing. May they expect to find no foes but only friends, no grief but only joy, and no shadow but only the splendour of your presence. So that we also may attain the resurrection of the just, keep our ears open to the call of duty, and our eyes closed to the seduction of evil; through our Saviour Jesus Christ.

NOW to the God of all grace, who has called us to his eternal glory by Jesus Christ, be praise and honour given, now and for ever.
        Amen

6

EASTER DAY

THE BIDDING

WE can rejoice and be full of confidence because Christ has been raised from the dead, and now lives and reigns in triumph to the end of time.

Let us pray:

WE praise you, O God the Father Almighty, for so wonderfully raising Jesus Christ from the dead.

We praise you, O God the Son, for breaking the power of evil and the grave.

We praise you, O God the Holy Spirit, for inspiring our hearts with the joy of Christ's resurrection.

To you, Father, Son and Holy Spirit, one God, be all praise and glory on this holy Easter Day.

HOLY heavenly Father, on this day of joy our sin is the only sadness; on this day of light our guilt is the only shadow. We confess that we live under a dark cloud and can only plead: 'God be merciful to us sinners'. We admit that we are not strangers to the sins which nailed Christ to the cross. Like the Pharisees, we have been self-righteous and resentful of criticism. Like Pilate we have been unjust and evaded our duty. And, like the disciples, we have been disloyal. But now, trusting in your love and in your unwearied patience with sinners, we ask for your pardon.

Lord have mercy
Christ have mercy
Lord have mercy

MAY our merciful God grant us forgiveness of our sins, time to amend our lives, and the grace and comfort of the Holy Spirit.

Amen

ALMIGHTY God, who, by the death and resurrection of Jesus Christ, removed the fetters of sin, throw open the gate of our prison and set us free. Forbid it that we should ever return to that bondage. But, resisting every temptation, and remaining free in spirit, may we love you with all our heart, and our neighbour also; for the sake of Jesus Christ our Saviour.

O LORD Jesus Christ, who, by rising from a sepulchre in Jerusalem, extended the splendour of your life over all mankind, grant us grace to walk and work in that radiance to the end of our days.

OUR FATHER ....

INTERCESSIONS

MERCIFUL God and heavenly Father, as we rejoice with Christians everywhere this Easter Day, we pray for the Church.

May the great company of believers find today that their faith grows stronger, and their service to others more eager. Today may they assist in extending your Kingdom throughout the world.

101

Lord in your mercy
Hear our prayer

GOD of love and grace, hear us as we pray for all whose hearts are sore because a dear one has died—and we think particularly of those who sorrow without faith or hope. Comfort them with the message of the resurrection: 'Your beloved are not here; they are risen'. And for the dying we pray, that they may be upheld by Christ's assurance: 'I am the resurrection and the life'.

Lord in your mercy
Hear our prayer

TO your loving care, O God, we commend those sufferers who feel crucified by disease, or wounded, as with a lance, by a painful ailment. Enable them to endure with a courageous faith drawn from him, who suffered for us on Calvary, even Jesus Christ our Lord.

Lord in your mercy
Hear our prayer

O GOD, whose eyes mark even the fall of a small sparrow, protect little children from sudden death in their cots, and guard others from danger in our busy streets.

Lord in your mercy
Hear our prayer

MOST gracious God, grant that the joy and hope and reassurance, which we—and countless others—draw from our worship today, may not be allowed to evaporate tomorrow, but may remain in us a continuing source of strength.

Lord in your mercy
Hear our prayer

GOD of eternity, we thank you for saints, apostles and martyrs, for heroes of the faith and pious benefactors, and for all humble people who have lived for you and their fellows. Keep us, Lord, in fellowship with the saints, until our time comes to leave those who are dying here, and join those who are living yonder, in the perpetual joy of your presence; through Jesus Christ our Lord.

AND to you our God, Father, Son and Holy Spirit, be honour, glory and praise, both now and evermore.

Amen

THANKSGIVING

Sursum Corda

Minister:	Lift up your hearts
All:	*We lift them to the Lord*
Minister:	Let us give thanks to the Lord our God
All:	*It is right to give him thanks and praise*

Let us pray:

IT is indeed right that we should at all times and in all places thank you, O Holy Lord, Father Almighty, Everlasting God, for all your loving kindness. But chiefly are we bound to praise you this day for the cross and resurrection of your Son, our Saviour Jesus Christ.

WE thank you that for us he endured the cruelty of men, the

agony of the Cross, and the gloom of the grave.

WE thank you that his redeeming work is done, his fight with evil over, and his battle won.

WE thank you that our Saviour, risen from the tomb, lives and reigns with you for ever. And therefore we praise you saying:

Glory be to the Father, and to the Son, and to the Holy Spirit, as it was in the beginning, is now and ever shall be, world without end.

Amen

7

WHIT SUNDAY

WHILE the day of Pentecost was running its course, they were all together in one place .... And they were all filled with the Holy Spirit.

The promise is to you, and to your children, and to all who are far away, everyone whom the Lord our God may call.

Let us pray:

ALMIGHTY and everlasting God, with the whole Christian Church we join this day in thanking you for pouring out your Spirit on the first disciples. We praise you that the Holy

Spirit has been given to the Church in every age, sanctifying both the worshippers and the sacraments, and enabling some to be preachers or prophets, teachers or leaders.

AS the Spirit came in wind and fire to the apostles, so may he come to us, breathing life into our souls, and kindling the fire of love in our hearts.

O HOLY God, in your presence we are conscious of our unworthiness. Time and again we have grieved your Spirit with our impure thoughts and angry feelings, our bad deeds done and good duties left undone. We confess that we have hindered the work of the Spirit by objecting to change, or dismissing new ideas. Most merciful God have mercy on us. Forgive our many faults, and help us to get rid of them; for the sake of your Son, our Saviour.

> *Lord have mercy*
> *Christ have mercy*
> *Lord have mercy*

HEAR God's promise of pardon through the mouth of his prophet: 'I have blotted out, as a thick cloud, your transgressions, and, as a cloud, your sins'. Thanks be to God.

HOLY Spirit of God, we pray that you will help us, and all other forgiven sinners.

From being economical with the truth;
From turning a deaf ear to the voice of conscience;
From turning a blind eye to the signal of duty;
    Deliver us, O Holy Spirit.

From rejecting the counsel of the wise;

From neglecting the means of grace;
From ignoring the example of the saints;
Deliver us, O Holy Spirit.

From calling evil something that is plainly good;
From darkening the light by which others see;
From discouraging the hearts of our fellow men;
Deliver us, O Holy Spirit.

OUR FATHER ....

INTERCESSIONS

ALMIGHTY and all-merciful God, send your Holy Spirit to assist us in the prayers we offer for the Church and the world.

MAINTAIN, O Lord, in vigorous life the Church of Christ. May this great tree, rooted in Calvary's hill, never cumber the ground and be cut down. Let its branches be a shelter to the weary and heavy-laden, and its leaves serve for the healing of the nations. In particular, we pray for your blessing on the Church in this land, so that it may grow, blossom and flourish to your glory.

Lord in your mercy
Hear our prayer

HEAVENLY Father, send the Holy Spirit, we pray, to strengthen those who dedicate themselves to your service at this time. May their words and works do good to others, and may their lives commend the Saviour they love and whose name they bear.

Lord in your mercy
Hear our prayer

LET your Holy Spirit, O God, control the emotions and guide the thoughts of the leaders of the nations. Banish all plans for armed conflict. Instead, persuade them to fight the common enemies of mankind—famine, poverty and disease.

Lord in your mercy
Hear our prayer

WE commend to you, O Lord, our country and its citizens, our Queen and her counsellors, all magistrates and judges. With the guidance of the Holy Spirit, may they establish our society in law and order, in fairness to all, and in kindly concern for the underprivileged.

Lord in your mercy
Hear our prayer

O GOD, whose Spirit guides us into all truth, may his presence be felt in schools, colleges and universities, so that students and teachers discover that science alone will not make them good, and that knowledge alone will not meet their deepest needs, or fill their hearts.

Lord in your mercy
Hear our prayer

LOOK after the sick, O Lord, especially those persons we know and are fond of; remove their pain, and restore them to health. If that should be your will.

Lord in your mercy
Hear our prayer

ETERNAL God, the strength of the redeemed, the joy of believers, and the life of the faithful departed, we rejoice in our fellowship with your saints. We thank you that they were inspired by the Holy Spirit to love you, and engage in battle the forces of evil. May we also fight the good fight, and daily increase in your Holy Spirit, more and more, until we come to your everlasting Kingdom.

Amen

8

TRINITY SUNDAY

THE grace of the Lord Jesus Christ, and the love of God, and fellowship in the Holy Spirit, be with you all.

Let us pray:

WE praise you, O God, the Father of us all, Creator of the world and all things in it, Giver of life and light.

WE praise you, O God the Son, Revealer of God to man, Guide of man to God, Saviour of our souls.

WE praise you, O God the Holy Spirit, Inspirer of goodness, Teacher of truth, Quickener of dead souls.

O HOLY and glorious Trinity, Father, Son and Holy Spirit, one true, eternal God, we praise you and magnify your holy Name.

O GOD, most holy, loving and merciful, in the light of your presence we are filled with awe, and made aware of our frailty and faults. We confess that we have disobeyed you, our Father; displeased our Lord Jesus Christ; and grieved the Holy Spirit. Pride has ruled our wills, and impurity has stained our minds. Slander has poisoned our tongues, and envy stirred our hearts. Humble and penitent we ask for your forgiveness.

Lord have mercy
Christ have mercy
Lord have mercy

MAY the almighty and merciful Lord grant *you* pardon and remission of all *your* sins, time for amendment of life, and the grace and comfort of the Holy Spirit.

Amen

JESUS said: 'Whoever does the will of my Father is my brother and sister'.

IT is the Will of God
    That we should love him with all our heart and our neighbour as ourself;
    That we should rule our spirits, and live peaceably with everyone.
    That we would pray for enemies, turn the other cheek and go a second mile.
        Lord, your will be done.

IT is the Will of God
>That we should not be anxious about tomorrow, or about food, drink and clothes;
>That we should not store up for ourselves treasure on earth;
>That we should set our mind on God's Kingdom and his justice before anything else.
>>*Lord, your will be done.*

OUR FATHER ....

INTERCESSIONS

ALMIGHTY God, by whose holy Apostle we are asked to pray for others, be pleased to hear our humble intercessions.

FOR your Church, O God, holy, catholic and apostolic, we pray that it may preserve the Faith once delivered to the saints. Send your Spirit to energise the Church for its work of preaching the Gospel, denouncing the wicked, defending the oppressed, seeking the lost, and persuading unbelievers to put their trust in you.

>*Lord in your mercy*
>*Hear our prayer*

FOR our country we pray, and for our gracious Queen and her councillors. Assist them—and us—to deal with the worst evils in the land, with child abuse, sexual perversion and drug addiction, with racism and widespread dishonesty in all ranks. Lay it on our minds that no nation can prosper and be happy, except under your law and favour.

Lord in your mercy
Hear our prayer

ALMIGHTY God, who made human life a trial of faith, character and courage, we pity and pray for those who have broken down under its stress. We remember also those who are stumbling, because they lack any spiritual support. Assure them all that your arms are open to welcome them, and that you can meet their need.

Lord in your mercy
Hear our prayer

BLESS, O Lord, the men and women who teach in our schools, colleges and universities. Helped by the Holy Spirit, may they cheerfully direct the country's youth into sound scholarship and good living.

Lord in your mercy
Hear our prayer

FOR those who shape public opinion on important matters, we pray that the Holy Spirit may guide their thinking, speaking and writing. And, O God, send the Spirit to direct and control those who provide entertainment, lest they offer us impurity and violence.

Lord in your mercy
Hear our prayer

ETERNAL God, blessed Trinity, we give thanks for your faithful and saintly servants of the past, and especially for those dear to our hearts, who would have ascribed any virtues they had to your grace. Gladden us by their memory, teach

111

us by their example, and comfort us with the hope that we shall be united with them in the life to come; through Jesus Christ our Lord, who lives and reigns with you, O Father, and the Holy Spirit, ever one God, world without end.

Amen

THANKSGIVING

Sursum Corda

Minister: Lift up your hearts
All: *We lift them to the Lord*
Minister: Let us give thanks to the Lord our God
All: *It is right to give him thanks and praise*

Let us pray:

ETERNAL God, most wise, holy and gracious, we praise you, who, for the sake of man's redemption, made yourself known as Father, Son and Holy Spirit, the one, true and living God.

WE thank you, O God the Father, for creating us in your own image, endowing us with the ability and freedom to become your children.

WE thank you, O God the Son, for coming down to a fallen world, and entering human life to teach us by word, and guide us by example, and rescue us by your sacrificial love.

WE thank you, O God the Holy Spirit, for breathing life into our souls, speaking to our conscience, and inspiring us to good thoughts and deeds.

112

TO you Father, Son and Holy Spirit, blessed and glorious
Trinity, be thanks and praise for ever and ever.

Amen

9

HARVEST THANKSGIVING

THE Lord said:
    While the earth lasts
    seedtime and harvest, cold and heat,
    summer and winter, day and night,
    shall never cease.
Thanks be to God.

Let us pray:

O LORD our God, Creator of all things, ruler of the chang-
ing seasons, and lord of the harvest, we worship you. Your
glory the heavens are telling. Your power the earth and the
sea declare. All your works praise you, O God.

    Lest we alone should be dumb, lift up our spirits to
gladness and praise; through Jesus Christ our Lord.

HEAVENLY Father, giver of breath and bread, provider of
fruits and flowers, only our sins can we call our own. With
shame we confess that we take your generosity for granted
and your gifts as our due. With sorrow we admit that we
have paid little attention to you from whom we get so much,

and have neglected our neighbours to whom we give so little.

O LORD, spare us that sad word: 'The harvest is past, the summer is ended, and we are not saved'. Therefore bring us now to a true repentance. And pardon our faults and frailties for the sake of our Saviour Jesus Christ.

Lord have mercy
Christ have mercy
Lord have mercy

O GOD, merciful and loving, forgive us all our sins, and raise us to new life in Jesus Christ our Lord.

O LORD our God, the king of creation, speak to us through the bountiful harvest and gathered fruits of garden and orchard. Assure us that your providence rules our lives from first to last, and shall never cease.

LORD, speak to us through the harvest which has followed seedtime. Warn us that we shall reap whatever we sow. Thus cautioned, may we more readily perform our duties, and more often ask the Holy Spirit to guide our thoughts and deeds.

LORD, speak to us through the empty stubble-fields and the falling leaves. Remind us that time is passing swiftly, and human life is brief, and heaven or hell awaits us all.

OUR FATHER ....

INTERCESSIONS

FATHER in heaven, hear us as we pray for other and needy members of your huge family.

FOR the members of the worldwide Church we pray, that all of them may be eager and ready to work for and support the Church, lest it be said: 'The harvest truly is plentiful, but the labourers are few'.

Lord in your mercy
Hear our prayer

FOR this congregation of your people we pray, that it may be like a field which you have blessed, where good seed is sown, where thorns and thistles are few, and where things that are pure, lovely and of good repute flourish and abound.

Lord in your mercy
Hear our prayer

FOR those who till the earth, who plough and sow and reap, we pray, that they may gather their crops at this season with gladness, and give thanks to you for your goodness.

Lord in your mercy
Hear our prayer

FOR our fishermen, who gather the harvest of the sea at the risk of their lives, we pray, that by skillful navigation they may ride out the storms and return to harbour safely, thanking you for your mercy.

Lord in your mercy
Hear our prayer

FOR the many millions of people who are underfed and emaciated, we pray. Prompt those, who enjoy plenty of good food and grow fat, to share their bread with the hungry and those dying of famine.

Lord in your mercy
Hear our prayer

FOR the great number of our contemporaries, we pray, whose souls are hungry, though they may not know it. Send the Holy Spirit to them, to convey the good news of Him who is the true Bread of Life, even Jesus Christ our Lord.

Lord in your mercy
Hear our prayer

ALMIGHTY God, we thank you for your saints, who have faithfully laboured in the field of human life and reaped a golden harvest. Encouraged by their example, may we have something to show at the last, and be carried, like sheaves of ripened corn, to our eternal home with you; through Jesus Christ our Lord, to whom, with you our Father, and the Holy Spirit, be glory and praise both now and for evermore.

Amen

THANKSGIVING

Sursum Corda

Minister:	Lift up your hearts
All:	*We lift them to the Lord*
Minister:	Let us give thanks to the Lord our God
All:	*It is right to give him thanks and praise*

Let us pray:

IT is indeed right to give you thanks and praise O God, the Creator of this vast world, and the sustainer of it through millions of years.

WE thank you for all the world's wonder, and for our much-loved native land, with its empty spaces, wind-blown grasses, high hills and heather.

WE thank you for the fertile ground, with fields tilled and planted for a harvest, and for orchards and gardens, and the colour, beauty and interest of flowers.

WE thank you for the Church, long-established in our towns and countryside, where Christ meets even the faithful two or three, and feeds our hungry souls with his gifts of Bread and Wine.

TO you, therefore, O Lord our God, and to Jesus Christ our Saviour, and to the Holy Spirit our Sanctifier, be thanks-giving and praise, now and for ever.   *Amen*

10

ALL SAINTS

THE BIDDING

LET us remember before God with thanksgiving the faithful of all ages; the patriarchs and prophets; the apostles, martyrs and confessors, who have lived throughout the centuries.

Let us pray:

ALMIGHTY and eternal God, we give you thanks and praise for all your saints, whom we gladly commemorate at this time.

Keep us in unbroken fellowship with your faithful servants of the past so that we, who are dedicated to the same cause that they nobly advanced, may serve you today with a similar devotion; for the sake of Jesus Christ our Lord.

O GOD, the King of saints and the Redeemer of sinners, we are not worthy to be numbered among the faithful. With their shining example before us, we are ashamed to think how dull and poor has been our performance.

We accuse ourselves
>of respecting the prophets but ignoring their teaching;
>of admiring the devotion of apostles and martyrs but making no sacrifice ourselves;
>of praising the saints continually but ignoring any call to help our fellow creatures.

Forgive, O Lord, our failure to live up to the best we know, and our refusal to aim at excellence.

Lord have mercy
Christ have mercy
Lord have mercy

MAY our merciful God forgive our sins, and strengthen us by his Holy Spirit to live a better life.

O GOD, by you the saints were strong to overcome their own weakness, and endure the opposition of the wicked, to you we also turn for help. Give us valour in place of our cowardice; wisdom in place of our folly; and virtue in place of our frailty.

O LORD Jesus Christ, who did your Father's will to the end with unflinching courage and complete trust, give us your Spirit, that we may continue your faithful servants and soldiers unto our life's end.

OUR FATHER ....

INTERCESSIONS

ALMIGHTY God, from whom saints draw their strength and grace, we offer our prayers for all people who, like us, need your help.

MERCIFUL Father, who in centuries past protected the Church, we pray for its welfare today. Assist the clergy and laity in this country to meet the challenge of a worldly and multi-racial society. Help us to convert the pagans and re-convert the deserters, and win over those of other faiths. In this way may our nation become more fully Christian.

Lord in your mercy
Hear our prayer

O GOD the King of peace, reign over all of us. Help the nations and their leaders to control their aggression. Beget in them thoughts of peace and not of war. Persuade them to take up arms against crime and incurable disease.

Lord in your mercy
Hear our prayer

LOVING Father, we pray that healing and comfort are given to those who suffer to a greater degree than most—the maimed and the blind, the deaf and dumb. And grant, O Lord that neurotic, senile and suicidal patients are nursed with great care and kindness.

Lord in your mercy
Hear our prayer

GOD of love and power, because we know you are willing to forgive, and able to mend what is broken, we pray
    for convicts and prisoners of justice;
    for thieves, scoundrels and men of violence;
    and for alcoholics and drug-addicts.
    Through the power of the Holy Spirit light the fire of conscience in them, and give them warmth to melt their hearts, and light to see the narrow way that leads to life.

Lord in your mercy
Hear our prayer

FATHER in heaven, we pray that your love, which is infinite and invincible, may surround and comfort the grieving parents of a dead, or disgraced child; and any lonely person who mourns a dear friend gone; and all aged persons whose only conversation is a lament for days of long ago.

Lord in your mercy
Hear our prayer

ETERNAL God, since your saints have made of human life a

pilgrim's progress on the way to glory, grant that we also may be travellers on that road. And, having left behind the City of Destruction, ignored the pleasure of Vanity Fair, and escaped from Giant Despair, may we overcome the other dangers and difficulties of our journey. Then, Lord, help us across the River of Death, and through the gates of the Celestial City; for the sake of Jesus Christ our Lord.

AND now to you, our God, whom the hosts of heaven worship everlastingly, we give honour, glory and praise, world without end.

Amen

THANKSGIVING

Sursum Corda

Minister:	Lift up your hearts
All:	*We lift them to the Lord*
Minister:	Let us give thanks to the Lord our God
All:	*It is right to give him thanks and praise*

Let us pray:

IT is indeed right to give you thanks and praise at all times, O Holy Lord, Father Almighty, Everlasting God.

AT this season especially we thank you for the saints of every age and every land;
> for Hebrew patriarchs, prophets and psalmists, who spoke, wrote and sang of you;
> and for the apostles who spread the Gospel far and wide,

121

and for the messengers who brought the Faith to our benighted shores.

AND we thank you, O Lord, for all who established and supported the Church in our land; for the famous and obscure; for men of remarkable gifts and plain, devoted people, who kept the spiritual lamp alight, even in the stormiest days.

GRANT, Lord, that the fellowship we have with the saints may assist us to remain steadfast in faith, and persistent in good works to the end of our days.

AND unto you, O Lord our God, be glory and praise for ever and ever.

Amen

11

REMEMBRANCE SUNDAY

THE BIDDING

WE are assembled here in solemn remembrance of the brave men and women, living and dead, who served our country faithfully in two great wars.

And we are here to give God thanks for his mercies to us then and now, and to promise that, so far as in us lies, the evil of war shall not happen again.

Let us pray:

ALMIGHTY and eternal God, we thank and praise you for all that you have done for us in time past. We thank you for saving us from the assault of our enemies, delivering us from many and great dangers, and raising up brave men and women to defend our country, many of whom gave to its cause the last full measure of devotion. With proud thanksgiving we will remember them.

HEAVENLY Father, we humbly acknowledge that we are not worthy of your mercy, or of the sacrifice made by others on our behalf. In us appear the sins which lead to war, and provoke you each day. We confess to pride and an aggressive spirit, to envy of others and greed for what they have. We condemn our enemies for their crimes, as if they were peculiar to them, while we ignore our own guilt. In shame and sorrow, we ask your forgiveness.

> *Lord have mercy*
> *Christ have mercy*
> *Lord have mercy*

MAY God in his mercy pardon what we have been,
    and repair what we are,
    and shape what we shall be;
for the sake of Jesus Christ, his Son, our Saviour.

ALMIGHTY God, as you have breathed in other and better men and women, who have been of good courage, fought the good fight, and kept the faith, so enter into us that we may live as Christ's faithful soldiers and servants, until our battle is done.

TEACH us, good Lord, to serve you as you deserve;
    to give and not to count the cost;

to fight and not to heed the wounds;
to toil and not to seek for rest;
to labour and to ask for no reward,
save that of knowing that we do your will;
through Jesus Christ our Lord.

(Ignatius Loyola: 1491-1556)

OUR FATHER ....

INTERCESSIONS

ALMIGHTY God, merciful and loving, we offer now our prayers of intercession.

IN your Kingdom, O God, no gun is fired; help us therefore to abolish the shooting and killing of human beings. Remind us all that we belong to the one human family which owns you as Father. And therefore rouse in us a sense of brotherhood which would make war impossible.

Lord in your mercy
Hear our prayer

WE pray, O Lord, for your continued favour to our country and Commonwealth. Bless our gracious Queen, her government, and those who keep order or administer justice. May the day come when we all shall enjoy a peaceful and contented life.

Lord in your mercy
Hear our prayer

GUIDE, O Lord, the eager and wayward youth of today. May

124

they not grow up to be cowardly and selfish, indifferent to world peace, and dismissive towards religion. May they grow rather into disciplined soldiers of Christ, marching under his banner to fight the forces of evil.

Lord in your mercy
Hear our prayer

WE commend to your care, O Lord, those who still bear the scars of warfare, or suffer for the loss of their limbs, or their sight, or their hearing. May they take pride today in being tried and valiant soldiers.

Lord in your mercy
Hear our prayer

O LORD Jesus Christ, we pray you, as the King and Head of the Church, to invigorate all its members and recover the backsliders. Support those who minister to your people in preaching the Gospel, teaching the young, and visiting the sick and needy. May they be saved from discouragement by the love in their hearts for you.

Lord in your mercy
Hear our prayer

ETERNAL God, the Inspirer of every good and useful life, we praise you for the noble army of martyrs, and the great company of your saints, among whom we number many good souls dear to us, whose warfare is accomplished and whose battle is won. Encouraged by their splendid example, may we follow, as they did, in the footsteps of Jesus Christ, the Captain of our salvation, until we reach your everlasting Kingdom.

NOW unto him who is able to keep us from falling, to the one and only God, our Saviour, be glory and majesty, dominion and power, for ever and ever.

Amen

THANKSGIVING

Sursum Corda

Minister:	Lift up your hearts
All:	*We lift them to the Lord*
Minister:	Let us give thanks to the Lord our God
All:	*It is right to give him thanks and praise*

Let us pray:

HEAVENLY Father, we thank and praise you for your kindness to us at all times and in all places. Your goodness never fails.

But on this day of Solemn remembrance, we offer you thanks in particular
> for your favour to our nation in time of war;
> for saving our land from invasion;
> for furnishing our table in the presence of our enemies;
> and for inspiring many to serve their country bravely and to die for their friends.

WITH proud thanksgiving we remember the great number who fought and fell in battle, whose bodies are buried at sea, or lie, far from home, in some foreign graveyard.

WE thank and praise you too, O God, for that even greater deliverance won for us by Jesus Christ, our Lord, who

126

defeated the forces of evil on the Cross, and won a glorious victory over sin and death.

NOW unto our God, who can give us the victory through our Lord Jesus Christ, be glory and praise, for ever and ever.

Amen

12

ST ANDREW'S DAY

OUR help is in the name of the Lord,
  maker of heaven and earth.

THE Lord our God be with us as he was with our fore-fathers; may he never leave us nor forsake us.

Let us pray:

BLESSED be God, the Father Almighty, the God of our fathers and our God. We worship and praise you, O Lord, for you have been the help and strength of your people in all generations. As we follow in their footsteps, may we also find that you will meet our every need, and that our chief end is to glorify you and enjoy you for ever; through Jesus Christ our Lord.

HOLY and merciful God, with sorrow and shame we acknowledge that we have sinned. We have long known your commandments, but have frequently broken them. We have heard the clear call of duty, but often ignored it. We have seen our neighbours in trouble, but too often have passed them by. And we also confess those sins to which we, as Scots, are prone—a stubborn pride, a native belligerence, and a long memory for past insults and injuries. For all our sins we humbly ask your pardon.

Lord have mercy
Christ have mercy
Lord have mercy

MAY our loving and merciful God forgive our sins, and help us to overcome our faults, through the grace of our Lord Jesus Christ and the power of the Holy Spirit.

ALMIGHTY God, who gave such grace to your apostle Andrew that he counted the sharp and painful death of the Cross to be a high honour and a great glory, grant us to take and esteem all troubles and adversities which shall come to us for your sake, as things profitable for our eternal salvation.

HEAVENLY Father, as you have given us a fine heritage in the name, history and traditions of Scotland, grant that we may guard that heritage and keep faith with our forefathers.

May there always be found in Scotland many men and women who will bring to their profession, or trade, high principles and honest labour, and to their Church loyalty and generous support;

For the sake of Jesus Christ our Lord.

OUR FATHER ....

INTERCESSIONS

FATHER in heaven, whose love embraces the whole human race, hear our prayers for others in the name of Jesus Christ. GOD bless the dedicated company of your people in all lands, and, in particular, in the Church of Scotland, the Church of the faith of our fathers. Preserve it in spiritual health. Prosper its work. And, as Andrew brought his brother and then others to Christ, so may our Church strive to draw those of our own country, and then strangers, into the fellowship of your Son.

Lord in your mercy
Hear our prayer

WE commend to your guidance, O Lord, all those in schools, colleges and universities. As the young grow in learning, so may they grow in wisdom. May they also increase in respect for the Church, and for what has been revealed to us through Christ our Saviour.

Lord in your mercy
Hear our prayer

MERCIFUL God, make yourself known in love and power to patients, doctors and nurses in our many hospitals, so that true Christian love may increase the skill of the staff, and assist the process of healing in the sick.

Lord in your mercy
Hear our prayer

ALMIGHTY God, the Judge and Saviour of us all, send, we pray, your Holy Spirit into our crowded prisons to make the wardens patient and kindly, and rouse the prisoners to penitence, and a resolve to start afresh as disciplined citizens.

Lord in your mercy
Hear our prayer

O GOD, our help in ages past, be today's helper of all our countrymen here in Scotland, and our kindred overseas. May the best qualities of our race appear in all of us. And ensure that the best traditions of our native land keep us honest, brave and loyal.

Lord in your mercy
Hear our prayer

O LORD our God, we remember with thanksgiving all who, in the long and colourful history of our country, fought nobly for freedom, and those who struggled to reform the Church, and those who glorified you in lives of simple goodness, based on your written Word in the Bible. Where they led in courage, honesty and godliness may we follow to the end of our days. Then, Lord, in your mercy receive us in heaven, that land of the loyal, home of the brave, and temple of the blest.

MERCIFUL Father, accept our prayers, for the sake of your Son, our Saviour Jesus Christ, to whom, with you and the Holy Spirit, be all praise and glory, for evermore.   *Amen*

THANKSGIVING

Sursum Corda

Minister: Lift up your hearts

All: *We lift them to the Lord*
Minister: Let us give thanks to the Lord our God
All: *It is right to give him thanks and praise*

Let us pray:

IT is right, most merciful God, that we should give you thanks and praise for everything, but chiefly for what you decided, dared and did for us through your Son, our Saviour Jesus Christ.

WE thank you, O God, at this time for our native land, where beauty lies on mountain and moor, glen and loch and island; the land where the bones of our fathers are buried, where stand the dwellings they built and named.

WE thank you also, O God, for our country's music and songs, its literature and art, its achievements in applied science; and for its strong and ancient love of freedom.

WE praise you, O God, for our patron saint, the holy apostle Andrew, whose cross upon our flag has been an inspiration. And for all the saints who spread the Gospel in this land: for Ninian and Columba, Aidan and Cuthbert, Bridget and Margaret.

FOR your countless gifts and your everlasting mercy, we thank and praise you, our God, both now and evermore.

Amen

13

LAST SUNDAY *of the* YEAR

THE BIDDING

THIS is a time to pause and then go forward;
    a time to remember and be sad;
    a time to recall many happy hours;
    a time to be grateful to God for the past;
and a time to ask for his blessing on the future.

Let us pray:

ALMIGHTY and eternal God, moons wax and wane but your love remains constant; every day and every year reaches an end, but your mercy lasts for ever, therefore we praise you with grateful hearts.

HEAVENLY Father, we bow before you in the shadow of a dying year; a year in which we have broken our vows, promised much and accomplished little, succeeded sometimes but failed too often. Each conscience has its own sad tale to tell of time misspent, talents unused, and duties neglected. Forgive us those sins we pray, O Lord. And forgive also our bitter complaints because certain selfish desires and dreams were denied us.

> *Lord have mercy*
> *Christ have mercy*
> *Lord have mercy*

MAY the almighty and merciful Lord grant *you* pardon and remission of all *your* sins, time for amendment of life, and the grace and comfort of the Holy Spirit.

Amen

ALMIGHTY God, by whose mercy we have been allowed to live through another year of our life, let not that experience pass without yielding its lessons.

TEACH us, from the mistakes we made, to be more humble and tolerant.

TEACH us, from the many blessings we have received, to be more grateful and kind.

TEACH us, from the sorrows we have suffered, to be more sympathetic and helpful.

O LORD Jesus Christ, who warned us not to go on storing up treasure on earth, reduce our longing to accumulate money and costly possessions. Increase in us a desire for those better things which moth and rust do not spoil, and thieves cannot steal.

OUR FATHER ....

INTERCESSIONS

ALMIGHTY and eternal God, to whom a thousand years are as a single day, hear our hasty prayers for the Church and the World.

TO your love and power we commend the congregations of

the Church. May they set aside any failures in the past year, and summon up their courage to tackle the duties that lie ahead. Stir the members to a new loyalty to Christ. And may they not let a day pass without winning a victory over the world, the flesh and the devil.

Lord in your mercy
Hear our prayer

FATHER in heaven, we pray for many millions in the world who are ill-fed, ill-clad, ill-housed and, many of them, illiterate. Lay this burden of misery on the conscience of those who have power to release enough food, or funds, to meet much of this need.

Lord in your mercy
Hear our prayer

FATHER, we pray also for the millions who are suffering;
    those shut off in hospitals and sickrooms;
    and those who are held in detention or refugee camps;
    and any whose homes are breaking up in anger and
    bitterness.
Send the Holy Spirit the Comforter to them.

Lord in your mercy
Hear our prayer

ATTEND, O Lord, to the aged and lonely, especially those who have have fallen on evil days, and feel that no one cares. And may the enfeebled and senile receive the watchful care and kindly, patient nursing they require.

Lord in your mercy
Hear our prayer

GUARD, O Lord we pray, all who travel in wintry conditions by road or rail, by sea or air. May no human error, or lack of concern for life, lead to an accident, and cause these travellers serious injury or sudden death.

Lord in your mercy
Hear our prayer

WE pray you, Lord, to fill our homes with your presence. And grant to family members who have gathered together at this time, health, happiness and kindly mirth; through the love and grace of Jesus Christ.

Lord in your mercy
Hear our prayer

GOD of eternity, King of saints, we rejoice that we have fellowship, here in this land of the dying, with the living who surround your throne in glory. May joy be with them, and may we all meet again; through Jesus Christ, your Son, our Saviour, to whom be praise and glory, world without end. *Amen*

THANKSGIVING

Sursum Corda

Minister:	Lift up your hearts
All:	*We lift them to the Lord*
Minister:	Let us give thanks to the Lord our God
All:	*It is right to give him thanks and praise*

Let us pray:

WE thank and praise you, O God, for bringing us in safety and good heart to the end of this year. You have been our joy in days of sunshine and our refuge when storms broke over our heads. You have been far kinder than we deserved, for which we shall be for ever grateful.

FOR guiding our steps and guarding our souls;
for preserving our health, and giving us friends;
We thank you, O God.

FOR comforting our sorrows and answering our prayers;
for giving us your grace and sheltering us in your Church;
We thank you, O God.

AS we ring out the old year and ring in the new, may we re-dedicate ourselves to your service. And to you, Father, Son and Holy Spirit, one God, blessed Trinity, we give thanks and praise now and evermore.

Amen

14

FUNERAL SERVICE—
For a CREMATORIUM

INTRODUCTORY SENTENCES:

THE eternal God is our refuge, and underneath are his everlasting arms. He comforts us in all our troubles, so that we in turn may be able to comfort others.

Wherefore let us worship God, and remember his presence with us now.

PRAISE: [A suitable hymn or psalm may be sung.]

WE are gathered together here in the faith of the life everlasting to thank God for our friend .... , whose soul he has summoned out of this present world into the peace and happiness of the next world.

WE are here also to seek God's comfort for ourselves and, especially, for those who knew and loved our friend best, and will therefore miss him/her most.

TRIBUTE: [Here may follow a brief acknowledgment of affection or esteem. It might end with these sentences from Thackeray's *Roudabout Papers*, or other helpful quotation.]

'Those who departed loving you, love you still, and you will love them always. They are not really gone, those dear hearts and true; they are only gone into the next room: and you will presently get up and follow them.'

SCRIPTURE READINGS:

AS a father pities his children, so the Lord pities those who fear him. For he knows our frame; he remembers that we are dust.

AS for man, his days are like grass, he flourishes like a flower of the field; for the wind passes over it, and it is gone, and its place knows it no more. But the steadfast love of the Lord is from everlasting to everlasting upon those who fear him, and his righteousness to children's children.

(Psalm 103, RSV)

THERE is hope of a tree, if it be cut down, that it will sprout again, and that its shoots will not cease .... But man dies, and is laid low .... If a man die, shall he live again?   (Job 14)

JESUS said: 'I am the resurrection and the life; he who believes in me, though he die, yet shall he live, and whosoever lives and believes in me shall never die. Do you believe this?'   (John 11)

LET not your hearts be troubled [said Jesus]; believe in God, believe also in me. In my Father's house are many rooms; if it were not so, would I have told you that I go and prepare a place for you? .... Let not your hearts be troubled, neither let them be afraid.   (John 14)

WHO shall separate is from the love of Christ? .... I am sure that neither death, nor life ... nor things present, nor things to come ... will be able to separate us from the love of God in Christ Jesus our Lord.   (Romans 8)

And I saw the holy city, new Jerusalem, coming down out of heaven from God ... and I heard a great voice from the throne saying, 'Behold the dwelling of God is with men. He will dwell with them, and they shall be his people, and God himself shall be with them; he will wipe away every tear from their eyes, and death shall be no more, neither shall there be mourning nor crying nor pain any more, for the former things have passed away ... and his servants shall worship him; they shall see his face, and his name shall be in their foreheads. And night shall be no more; they need no light of lamp or sun, for the Lord God will be their light, and they shall reign for ever and ever.

(Revelation 21 and 22)

Thanks be to God

Let us pray:

ETERNAL God, from of old you have been our refuge in trouble or sadness and never failed us; we praise you for your unwearied love and care. At all times, but never more than now in the shadow of death, we thank you for your Son Jesus Christ. We are glad and grateful that he became man for our salvation, and walked this ordinary earth, enduring the pain and brevity of human life, and at the end trod this dark valley of death, giving us comfort by his sorrow and life eternal by his death. We bless you for his Cross and Resurrection, and for the assurance that nothing—not even death—can ever separate us from your love.

O KING of saints, we praise you for all the good and true, the loyal and brave, who in this life served you and helped other people, and have gone before us into your heavenly Kingdom.

IN particular we thank you for your servant whose passing we now mourn. We remember with gladness his/her steadfast character ... generous and happy spirit ... gifts of nature and of grace ... courage in illness ... all that he/she was to the Church, to the circle of his/her friends ....

WE thank you, O Father, for one more good fight finished, one more pilgrim journey ended in heavenly places, one more child of yours gone safely home.

GOD of love and pity, you can heal every broken heart, therefore minister to those here who mourn a loved one with a sore sense of loss. Wipe away their tears. Comfort them with happy memories. And persuade them that you are doing now for their dear one all that they would do, if they could, and much more.

AND now as we do this last loving duty for a dear departed friend, grant us that peace of mind which you alone can give; through Jesus Christ our Lord, to whom, with you the Father, and the Holy Spirit, be all glory and praise, world without end.

Amen

THE COMMITTAL: [All standing.]

THE souls of the righteous are in the hands of God and no torment shall touch them.

FOR as much as it has pleased Almighty God to take to himself the soul of this our brother/sister departed, we therefore commit his/her body to its last resting place, ashes to ashes, dust to dust, in sure and certain hope of the life everlasting.

> GO forth upon your journey, Christian soul.
> GO in the name of God, the omnipotent Father, who created you.
> GO in the name of Jesus Christ, Son of the living God, who bled for you.
> GO in the name of the Holy Spirit, who breathed life into your soul.

And may your place today be found in peace.

Amen

PRAISE: [A suitable hymn may be sung]

THE BLESSING

15

The LORD'S PRAYER

OUR Father which art in heaven,
Hallowed be Thy name.
Thy Kingdom come.
Thy will be done in earth, as it is in heaven.
Give us this day our daily bread.
And forgive us our debts, as we forgive our debtors.
And lead us not into temptation, but deliver us from evil:
For Thine is the Kingdom, and the power, and the glory,
> for ever. *Amen*

OUR Father, which art in heaven,
Hallowed be Thy name.
Thy Kingdom come.
Thy will be done in earth as it is in heaven.
Give us this day our daily bread.
And forgive us our trespasses, as we forgive them that
> trespass against us.
And lead us not into temptation, but deliver us from evil:
For Thine is the Kingdom, the power, and the glory, for
> ever and ever. *Amen*

(REVISED TRADITIONAL VERSION)

OUR Father who art in heaven,
hallowed be thy Name,
thy Kingdom come,
thy will be done;
on earth as it is in heaven.
Give us this day our daily bread.
And forgive us our trespasses,
as we forgive those who trespass against us.
And lead us not into temptation;
but deliver us from evil.
For thine is the Kingdom,
and the power, and the glory,
for ever and ever. *Amen*

16

The APOSTLES' CREED

I BELIEVE in God the Father Almighty, Maker of heaven and earth;

And in Jesus Christ His only Son our Lord, Who was conceived by the Holy Ghost, Born of the Virgin Mary, Suffered under Pontius Pilate, Was crucified, dead, and buried; He descended into hell;

The third day He rose again from the dead; He ascended into heaven, And sitteth on the right hand of God the Father Almighty; From thence He shall come to judge the quick and the dead.

I believe in the Holy Ghost; The holy Catholic Church; The Communion of Saints; The Forgiveness of sins; The Resurrection of the body; And the Life everlasting.

Amen